W9-DBV-540

High-risk Students and Higher Education:
Future Trends

by Dionne J. Jones and Betty Collier Watson

ASHE-ERIC Higher Education Report 3, 1990

Prepared by

Clearinghouse on Higher Education
The George Washington University

In cooperation with

Association for the Study
of Higher Education

Published by

School of Education and Human Development
The George Washington University

Jonathan D. Fife, Series Editor

ALVERNO COLLEGE
INSTRUCTIONAL SERVICES CENTER

Cite as

Jones, Dionne J., and Betty Collier Watson. 1990. *High-risk Students and Higher Education: Future Trends.* ASHE-ERIC Higher Education Report No. 3. Washington, D.C.: The George Washington University, School of Education and Human Development.

Library of Congress Catalog Card Number 90-060887
ISSN 0884-0040
ISBN 1-878380-00-1

Managing Editor: Bryan Hollister
Manuscript Editor: Barbara Fishel/Editech
Cover design by Michael David Brown, Rockville, Maryland

The ERIC Clearinghouse on Higher Education invites individuals to submit proposals for writing monographs for the *ASHE-ERIC Higher Education Report* series. Proposals must include:
1. A detailed manuscript proposal of not more than five pages.
2. A chapter-by-chapter outline.
3. A 75-word summary to be used by several review committees for the initial screening and rating of each proposal.
4. A vita and a writing sample.

ERIC **Clearinghouse on Higher Education**
School of Education and Human Development
The George Washington University
One Dupont Circle, Suite 630
Washington, DC 20036-1183

This publication was prepared partially with funding from the Office of Educational Research and Improvement, U.S. Department of Education, under contract no. ED RI-88-062014. The opinions expressed in this report do not necessarily reflect the positions or policies of OERI or the Department.

EXECUTIVE SUMMARY

Attrition is a major problem for American colleges and universities, and efforts to retain students are stymied and made complex because an increasing number of enrollees fit the socioeconomic and demographic profile of "high-risk" students. This issue is critical for the nation as a whole, because the increasing enrollment of high-risk students—minorities, females, and low-income and disabled individuals—is expected to continue into the 21st century.

High-risk students have a major impact on both institutions of higher education and society in general. Specifically, attrition affects patterns of funding, planning for facilities, and the long-term academic curricula of institutions of higher education. Attrition affects the future labor market, because students are unprepared for the required roles and responsibilities.

What causes attrition and risk? The answer to this seemingly simple question is rather complex. Indeed, a number of academic, nonacademic, and related factors are associated with attrition and risk. Academically, it appears that all students do not receive equal preparation in elementary and secondary schools. Moreover, the instructional approaches used by teachers of high-risk students tend to be inefficient. On the other hand, nonacademic factors associated with attrition and risk are generated by both teachers and students. For instance, teachers' negative attitudes affect students' self-esteem. Thus, many high-risk students develop low self-esteem and begin to cooperate with systemic forces resulting in pregnancy, dropping out, and delinquency.

To achieve success among high-risk students by the 21st century, a variety of strategies must be implemented. Special retention needs of high-risk students must be identified, and simultaneously, institutions must be committed to providing both financial and academic support. In addition, social support through advising and counseling from faculty, the family, and peers is a necessary part of this equation.

Are High-risk Students and Nontraditional Students the Same?

Although the characteristics of high-risk students are sometimes correlated with those of nontraditional students, the two concepts have different denotations. The term "high risk" is a theoretical concept based on an implicit assessment of the degree of negative risk associated with the educational experience. "High-risk students" are minorities, the academically disadvantaged, the disabled, and those of low socioeconomic status. "Nontraditional students," on the other hand, is merely a reference to the changing profile of students that emerged during the late 1960s and early 1970s as a result of demographic and sociopolitical change. Thus, nontraditional students typically include older adults, minorities, and individuals of low socioeconomic status. Some nontraditional students are not high-risk students, and, conversely, some high-risk students are traditional students. By the same token, some high-risk students are also nontraditional; for example, an older (or mature) student might also be academically underprepared.

What Is the Impact of High-risk Students on Institutions of Higher Education?

Full-time enrollments are critical to an institution's continued survival, and high levels of attrition adversely affect an institution's funding, facilities planning, and long-term planning for the curriculum. Declining enrollments, for instance, leave unused building capacity. Large numbers of part-time or academically underprepared students increase the average cost per student. Furthermore, high rates of noncompletion among others in the general student body magnify the problem. Some institutions have expanded their curricula to include special courses for their high-risk students. While some changes in curriculum have been directly related to colleges' and universities' efforts to reduce attrition, other changes have been indirect. For example, the majors that students choose and the changes they make in majors affect the development of curricula. Similarly, academically underprepared students who choose majors they perceive as less academically challenging affect the development of curricula, because as the university enrolls fewer students choosing "difficult" majors and more students choosing "easy" majors, its curriculum becomes thus shaped over time.

Are High-risk Students Treated Differently in Elementary and Secondary Schools?

To understand high-risk students in institutions of higher education, one must review the different experiences of students in elementary and high schools. The school curriculum seems to benefit white males and students of high socioeconomic status more than minorities, females, and students of low socioeconomic status (Reyes and Stanic 1985). For the most part, minorities, females, and students of low socioeconomic status begin their school experience with positive attitudes. But differences in race, gender, and social class often begin to emerge during elementary school and increase by high school and college. Discrimination based on class, race, and gender influences the quality and quantity of material taught in schools.

In the first place, the facilities and resources in high-income school districts are far superior to those in low-income school districts. Second, particularly in large metropolitan schools, African-American and other minority students are disproportionately placed in lower ability groups (or "tracks") with little prospect of advancing to higher ones. Even more alarming, the content of courses in academic subjects is often different from that offered to students in other tracks. For example, students in lower tracks may take general mathematics and science rather than algebra, trigonometry, biology, and chemistry (College Entrance Examination Board 1985).

Do Instructional Styles Vary in Classrooms?

Even within the classroom, some teachers vary their instructional styles depending on students' racial and socioeconomic status. Minority and poor children tend to be taught more by rote and repetition and less by questioning and intellectual discourse. White students and others of high socioeconomic status are trained in developing higher-order skills critical for solving problems. Such differences in instructional styles may place primary and secondary teachers in complicity with those forces leading to academic underpreparedness and attrition. African-Americans are a case in point. The achievement gap between African-Americans and whites begins in elementary school and widens as students advance along the educational pipeline through graduate school. With respect to that gap, the controversy surrounding testing and minorities has not yet been settled. It is still not clear just how much of the variance in measured academic achievement is a consequence of culturally biased tools.

Do Teachers' Negative Attitudes Adversely Affect Students' Self-esteem and Performance?

Schools are an umbrella system or organization from which discrimination and differential treatment are often meted out.

Subtle forms of discrimination can serve to undermine students' self-esteem and ultimately facilitate attrition. As a result of the social stratification in society, teachers and administrators may inherit a reality that creates an aversion to high-risk, low-income, and minority students. This internalization is then reflected in their attitudes and behavior toward those students.

Many scholars have confirmed the operation of a race-based ontology in the classroom. Teachers and others tend to separate children into "good" and "bad" students, with the polarized categories often based on race/ethnicity, gender, and class. These negative attitudes may result in prejudgment or avoidance of, for example, culturally different students to the point where students receive little or no academic or personal assistance. Such negative behaviors can lead to low aspirations and low self-esteem. And low self-esteem can in time cause students to "cooperate" with systemic forces and participate in various forms of antisocial behavior.

What Conclusions Are Reached and What Implications Can Be Drawn?

Students in institutions of higher education encounter risks in several forms. For example, risk might involve a higher probability of a low grade point average and/or a greater chance of not completing a college degree. It might also involve a relatively greater probability of choosing a field that is incongruent with the skills and competencies needed by the present labor market—and particularly by the labor market of the 21st century. The potential for risk and attrition exists for all college enrollees, but for some subgroups, the probability of risk and attrition is extraordinarily high.

A number of causal variables interact to increase attrition and risk among particular demographic and socioeconomic populations. These variables can include academic factors (low grade point average, academic underpreparedness, for example) but could extend far beyond the scope of the academic. Indeed, each high-risk student represents the outcome of his or her individual characteristics, combined with the shaping and contouring that occur as a consequence of a socially stratified society.

Regardless of the reason, however, attrition and risk are costly to the individual and to society, both directly and indirectly. Thus, strategies for intervention must be developed and implemented on a number of levels. Among students, high-risk students must be challenged to develop academic and nonacademic skills and competencies associated with success in college. At the institutional level, administrators, teachers, and counselors must engage in behaviors that facilitate persistence and completion of the program. In addition, institutions of higher education must make a financial commitment to high-risk students in the form of guaranteed financial assistance for the duration of their degree program. At the community level, businesses and community-based organizations have formed partnerships with educational institutions to reduce risk.

In addition to these strategies for achieving success among high-risk students, academic support services must be offered that include developing and building skills. Further, the provision of social support is vital. It can come from advisers/counselors, faculty, parents, family, and other students and peers. This framework brings together the student, the teacher, the institution, parents, peers, and the community in a dynamic synthesis.

ADVISORY BOARD

Alberto Calbrera
Arizona State University

Carol Everly Floyd
Board of Regents of the Regency Universities System
State of Illinois

Judy Gappa
San Francisco State University

George Keller
University of Pennsylvania

J. Fredericks Volkwein
State University of New York

Bobby Wright
Pennsylvania State University

Ami Zusman
University of California

CONSULTING EDITORS

Walter R. Allen
University of California

Leonard L. Baird
University of Kentucky

James H. Banning
Colorado State University

Trudy W. Banta
University of Tennessee

Margaret J. Barr
Texas Christian University

Louis W. Bender
Florida State University

Rita Bornstein
University of Miami

Larry Braskamp
University of Illinois

L. Leon Campbell
University of Delaware

Robert F. Carbone
University of Maryland

Susan Cohen
Lesley College

John W. Creswell
University of Nebraska

Mary E. Dilworth
ERIC Clearinghouse on Teacher Education

James A. Eison
Southeast Missouri State University

Valerie French
American University

J. Wade Gilley
George Mason University

Milton Greenberg
American University

Judith Dozier Hackman
Yale University

Brian L. Hawkins
Brown University

Joseph V. Julian
Syracuse University

Oscar T. Lenning
Robert Wesleyan College

Jeanne M. Likens
Ohio State University

Dierdre A. Ling
University of Massachusetts

James W. Lyons
Stanford University

Judith B. McLaughlin
Harvard University

Sherry Magill
Washington College

Andrew T. Masland
Digital Equipment Corporation

Christopher B. Morris
Davidson College

Yolanda T. Moses
California State University

Bernard Murchland
Ohio Wesleyan University

Michael T. Nettles
University of Tennessee

Elizabeth M. Nuss
National Association of Student Personnel Administrators

Edward H. O'Neil
Duke University

Jeffrey H. Orleans
Council of Ivy Group Presidents

Robert L. Payton
Indiana University

Joseph F. Phelan
University of New Hampshire

James J. Rhatigan
Wichita State University

Steven K. Schultz
Westmont College

Mary Ellen Sheridan
Ohio State University

Robert L. Sizmon
Wake Medical Center

Charles U. Smith
Florida Agricultural and Mechanical University

William F. Stier, Jr.
State University of New York at Brockport

Betty Taylor
Lesley College

Reginald Wilson
American Council on Education

REVIEW PANEL

Charles Adams
University of Amherst

Richard Alfred
University of Michigan

Philip G. Altbach
State University of New York

Louis C. Attinasi, Jr.
University of Houston

Ann E. Austin
Vanderbilt University

Robert J. Barak
State Board of Regents

Alan Bayer
Virginia Polytechnic Institute and State University

John P. Bean
Indiana University

Louis W. Bender
Florida State University

Carol Bland
University of Minnesota

Deane G. Bornheimer
New York University

John A. Centra
Syracuse University

Arthur W. Chickering
George Mason University

Jay L. Chronister
University of Virginia

Mary Jo Clark
San Juan Community College

Shirley M. Clark
University of Minnesota

Darrel A. Clowes
Virginia Polytechnic Institute and State University

Robert G. Cope
University of Washington

John W. Creswell
University of Nebraska

Richard Duran
University of California

Larry H. Ebbers
Iowa State University

Kenneth C. Green
University of Southern California

Edward R. Hines
Illinois State University

George D. Kuh
Indiana University

James R. Mingle
State Higher Education Executive Officers

Michael T. Nettles
University of Tennessee

Pedro Reyes
University of Wisconsin

H. Bradley Sagen
University of Iowa

CONTENTS

FOREWORD

The concern over high risk students is rooted in a concern for the futures of both our society and our higher education institutions. High risk students are those students who are intellectually capable and who, through no fault of their own, have been denied some of the advantages granted most of the current college-going students. These advantages include growing up in a loving, supportive nuclear family; having adequate financial resources or the credit rating to acquire financial resources; attending elementary and secondary school systems that provided adequate education; being influenced by a social culture that values education; having the physical abilities—such as adequate hearing, eyesight and mobility—to function in physical surroundings which are unforgiving to the physically disabled. In other words high risk students are those with a potential for achieving a higher education degree but who have a higher than average probability of not reaching their potential.

The concern for the future of our society is warranted by statistics which clearly evidence a large increase in minority youths and a decrease in youths from advantaged families. If our society is to maintain the quality of life that has developed since World War II, it must develop an educated citizenry that can adequately function within the increasingly global and technological world.

The concern for high risk students is also an act of self-interest for higher education institutions now feeling the effects of a rapid decrease in the traditional-aged student. An increasingly large percentage of this age cohort is made up of high risk students. As higher education institutions find that they have saturated the market for the older and non-traditional student, they must look to the high risk student to make up the difference. This does not mean that institutions must lower their academic standards, but they must change some basic expectations. For example, high risk students may take longer than the traditional four years to graduate. They may need special considerations to overcome basic learning disabilities, or be provided with some non-academic services currently not available. Institutions must change their mission from ensuring that the bright and the fortunate continue to be advantaged, to nurturing the potentials of those less advantaged.

In this report by Dionne J. Jones, Senior Research Associate, and Betty Collier Watson, Senior Research Economist, both at the National Urban League, Inc., answer some very important questions concerning high risk students. Questions such as "Who are high risk students?," "What are the important academic and nonacademic factors associated with attrition and risk?," and "What are the strategies that will be useful in achieving success among high risk students?"

The concern for high risk students has reached a state where many institutions believe they have some role to play in ensuring their success. This definitive review provides a foundation of information that will help turn this belief into reality.

Jonathan D. Fife
Series Editor
Professor of Higher Education and Director
ERIC Clearinghouse on Higher Education
The George Washington University

ACKNOWLEDGMENTS

We acknowledge our families, whose loving support and dedication continue to inspire and motivate us. We express gratitude to our students, many of whom can be categorized as high risk but who have persevered and survived the odds. We are most grateful to the National Urban League, John E. Jacob, president, Frank Lomax, III, executive vice president, and Billy J. Tidwell, director of research, for their inspired leadership. The National Urban League continues to strive tirelessly for the amelioration of racism in America and the pursuit of social justice.

The entire staff of the National Urban League's Washington office have supported our efforts, and we express our thanks. Dr. Tidwell offered provocative comments and constructive criticism, for which we are thankful. Monica L. Jackson, our colleague and friend, read parts of the draft and offered valuable insights. We thank her. And we are especially grateful to Kathleen Daily, Marcia Taylor, Deborah Searcy, and Caroline Badimo for their professional secretarial support, without which this manuscript would not be possible. Last, a special thanks to Sister Kathleen Feeley, president, College of Notre Dame of Maryland, for her untiring efforts to recruit and retain high-risk students.

INTRODUCTION

Over recent years, an abundance of research has emerged regarding the issue of retention and its converse, risk and attrition. Scholars have presented theories regarding the magnitude, nature, and causes of the problems that lead to students' failure to complete their objectives for higher education. Colleges and universities have become involved in institutional research designed to measure the phenomenon of risk and attrition as these forces operate within their individual organizations. Policy makers have commissioned a number of studies that appraise risk and attrition as these variables affect the overall character of higher education in the contemporary world.

Efforts to analyze risk and attrition have been driven by the practical as well as the ideational. Thus, theory and research have resulted in the formulation of initiatives and programs designed for the amelioration of risk and attrition. Budgetary priorities have included allocations of limited resources in support of needed strategies to reduce risk. And, in some cases, program evaluations have been skewed to ensure the continuation of funding.

Nevertheless, the problem of risk and attrition persists. Administrators are becoming increasingly uncertain of the financial wisdom of continued support of policies and programs for high-risk students. Increasingly, teachers are meeting to share grievances and complaints regarding the difficulties of instructing such students. Counselors are beginning to question the value of their efforts at intervention. And the general public is beginning to openly and actively call for a retreat from efforts to recruit and retain high-risk students.

But retreat is not a viable solution. The market for higher education is no longer a seller's market. Thus, colleges and universities need high-risk populations to ensure adequate levels of enrollment. Additionally, the labor market needs a highly skilled and trained work force to forestall a shortage of labor. And society needs the higher tax income, lower crime rates, and general educational literacy that accompany a well-educated populace. Thus, it is time to reexamine both theory and practice regarding risk and attrition; this report is intended to provide such a reevaluation.

As one surveys the myriad studies and reports on risk and attrition that have emerged over the last decade alone, it becomes clear that sufficient research and data are available for use by administrators in fine-tuning existing strategies. It is further apparent that two voids exist in the literature. First, theory and data that place risk and attrition in institutions of higher education within the framework of the broader problems confronting demographic and socioeconomic groups who are most at risk are in short supply. That is, the links between attrition and risk and various elements of social stratification within the United States are not apparent. Second, existing research does not adequately link risk and attrition in colleges and universities with practices, behaviors, and levels of risk in elementary and secondary schools. This report seeks to integrate knowledge from these two areas into the broader body of literature on risk and attrition.

THE CONCEPT OF HIGH-RISK STUDENTS:
Profiles and Characteristics

The topics covered in this section are quite complex. First, the section revisits the phenomenon of the "high-risk"[1] student. This concept, which was quite popular during the seventies, fell into academic disrepute during the eighties as analysts debated the relative merits and demerits of such nomenclature. Nevertheless, such groups do still exist; all demographic groups do not have equal chances of educational success.

... substantial evidence ... had placed [institutions of higher education] in complicity with the perpetuation of social and economic disadvantage.

Second, the section focuses on high-risk or at-risk students in institutions of higher education. That focus is narrow as it does not deal with other aspects of risk that characterize an individual's life in a socially stratified society. Thus, high-risk populations in institutions of higher education are, in a broad sense, extensions of high-risk populations in the society as a whole—females, minorities, the disabled, and the economically disadvantaged. Although this analysis is restricted to institutions of higher education, factors that elevate risk at this level often begin in the primary and secondary grades. Furthermore, risk extends beyond the undergraduate years into life's subsequent experiences.

Third, the admission of at-risk groups into a college or university poses a number of challenges for the institution. It has been well documented that institutions of higher education, like other institutions, share an organizational culture that is most often based on values, attitudes, and beliefs compatible to the survival of more "traditional" students. Thus, a discussion of high-risk students in higher education implicitly addresses a praxis that operates within the context of the "invisible tapestry" of institutions of higher education (Kuh and Whitt 1988).

Finally, a discussion of high-risk students must explicitly address the concrete programs and strategies that have been designed to enhance the probability of equality of educational outcomes. Preliminary to such discussion, however, is the more basic task of examining the emergence and use of the terms "high-risk student" and its suggested synonym, "nontraditional student."

---

1. The term "high risk" denotes any student whose probability of attrition is above average, and some scholars have viewed it as pejorative. The term as used in this monograph is used descriptively, with the acknowledged recognition of its negative connotation.

Nontraditional Students: The Context

The sixties catalyzed change in a number of America's institutions. The passage of federal legislation regarding minorities and females, the launching of the War on Poverty, and a more general shift of values in the American society emphasized not merely equality of outcomes but also equality of opportunity.

Given the critical historical role of education as a vehicle of social mobility, it is not surprising that educational institutions in general were profoundly affected by these changes. National, state, and local policy makers drastically increased educational expenditures. From 1960 to 1970, aggregate school expenditures increased from $23.9 billion to $68.5 billion (see table 1). After 1970, however, the rate of increase was much lower. From 1970 to 1980, educational expenditures increased from $68.5 billion to $165.6 billion—an increase of nearly 142 percent. From 1980 to 1988, total school expenditures increased to $308.8 billion—an increase of 86 percent (U.S. Dept. of Commerce 1989).

TABLE 1

TOTAL AGGREGATE SCHOOL EXPENDITURES: 1960, 1970, 1980, 1988

Year	Billions of Dollars	Percent Change
1960	23,860	–
1970	68,459	+186.9
1980	165,627	+141.9
1988	308,800	+86.4

Source: U.S. Dept. of Commerce 1989, table no. 200, p. 125.

Institutions of higher education disproportionately benefited from the increased funding. From 1960 to 1970, expenditures for colleges and universities rose by over 253 percent. The corresponding figures for the subsequent periods were 147 percent and 98 percent (see table 2). Similarly, institutions of higher education were viewed as pivotal in the efforts to extend equal opportunity to historically disadvantaged groups. Indeed, substantial evidence documents the charge that educational institutions' previous practices had placed them in complicity with the perpetuation of social and economic disadvantage (Gordon 1987).

TABLE 2

TOTAL AGGREGATE INSTITUTIONAL EXPENDITURES: 1960, 1970, 1980, 1988

Year	Billions of Dollars	Percent Change
1960	7,147	–
1970	25,276	+253.6
1980	62,465	+147.1
1988	124,000	+ 98.5

Source: U.S. Dept. of Commerce 1989, table no. 200, p. 125.

Institutions of higher education moved toward compliance with the new moral and legislative mandates. Several colleges and universities established flexible admission standards designed to increase the participation of minorities, females, and other disadvantaged students in higher education. Of note are the efforts of Florida's community colleges and universities and the University of California at Davis's special action student program (Bender and Blanco 1987; Hunziker 1987).

In the aggregate, such efforts were successful. In 1960, only 3.1 percent of African-Americans had completed four or more years of college, but the percentage increased to 4.1 percent by 1970, 8.4 percent by 1980, and 10.7 percent by 1987. The comparable figures for Hispanics were 4.5 percent, 7.6 percent, and 8.6 percent in 1970, 1980, and 1987, respectively. The growth among females in higher education was even more striking. In 1970, for example, only 8.4 percent of white females had completed four years or more of college. By 1987, the figure had more than doubled, to 16.9 percent (see table 3). Thus, colleges and universities not only increased equality of opportunity but also enhanced the equality of outcomes.

The mandate for increased opportunity, however, does not fully account for the increased numbers of minorities and women holding college degrees. The changing demographic profile of the country was also a propelling force. In 1970, for instance, 42.9 percent of all white male high school graduates were enrolled in college. By 1980, that figure had dropped to 34.3 percent, and in 1986, it had increased to only 36.1 percent. Further, in 1970, a plurality of college enrollees were males and females aged 18 to 24. By 1980, 34.3 percent of all enrollees were over 25 years of age, and by 1986, that proportion had increased to 38.6 percent. In addition, in 1970, only 14.2 percent of all students were enrolled in two-year

TABLE 3

YEARS OF COLLEGE COMPLETED BY RACE, HISPANIC ORIGIN, AND SEX: 1960, 1970, 1980, 1988

Year	Percent with Four or More Years of College	Percent Change
African-Americans		
1960	3.1	–
1970	4.1	+ 32
1980	8.4	+105
1987	10.7	+ 27
Hispanics		
1970	4.5	–
1980	7.6	+ 69
1987	8.6	+ 13
White Females		
1970	8.4	–
1980	13.3	+ 58
1987	16.9	+ 27

Source: U.S. Dept. of Commerce 1989, table nos. 211 and 212, pp. 130 and 131.

institutions, and only 28.4 percent of all students were part time. By 1986, more than 37.3 percent of all college students were in two-year institutions, and 43 percent of all college students were enrolled part time in two- and four-year institutions (U.S. Dept. of Commerce 1989). The clients of higher education had changed. The traditional profile of a college student had changed. Thus, the new profile came to be viewed as "nontraditional students" (Cohen and Brauer 1982).

Eventually, "nontraditional students" came to be viewed as synonymous with "high-risk students." Moreover, the traits of nontraditional students—women, minorities, adults, and part-time students—were correlated with those of students who have a high probability of not completing their college degrees, that is, high-risk students (Astin 1975). Thus, changing demographics and the increased efforts to create equal opportunity interacted to produce a new set of clients for institutions of higher education. In their efforts to sort through these complexities, analysts began categorizing students by the new typologies, "nontraditional" and "high risk."

Nontraditional versus High-risk Students

The concepts of nontraditional and high-risk students raise a number of questions. What are the characteristics of high-risk students? What are the characteristics of nontraditional students? And, most important, to what degree do these two categories overlap?

Characteristics of high-risk students

As mentioned, the efforts of colleges and universities to extend the benefits of higher education to historically disadvantaged groups were, on the whole, successful. The numbers of historically disadvantaged groups receiving college degrees dramatically increased. But new disparities in the educational process emerged between historically disadvantaged groups and traditional students.

First, it became apparent that, independent of the definition of attrition used, a disproportionate number of the "new" students did not complete their degrees and/or did not accomplish the objective that led to their initial enrollment (Tinto 1975). That is, from 1970 to 1987, the increase in the percentage of those racial and ethnic minorities with one to three years of college exceeded the rate of increase for those with four years or more of college. For example, the proportion of African-Americans with one to three years of higher education in 1987 was 166 percent higher than in 1970. The proportion of African-Americans with four years or more of college was only 136 percent higher than in 1970, however (U.S. Dept. of Commerce 1989). Similar trends characterized the educational experience of Hispanics and females. In other words, students were beginning but not completing college.

Institutional research documents such a trend. In 1985, the "special admits" at the University of California at Davis consisted of approximately 50 percent disadvantaged whites and 50 percent minority students (Hunziker 1987). The attrition rates for these students exceeded the rates for regular students. That is, more special admits than regular admits were characterized by a higher probability of dropping out with one to three years of college. Similarly, approximately 40 percent of students entering a four-year college never received a degree, and between 60 and 70 percent of students entering a two-year college never received a degree (Cope 1978).

In the second place, the educational experiences of these new students differed in terms of both risk of attrition and

risk of lower grade point averages (GPAs). A study of students enrolled at Florida's community colleges found that those students admitted on the basis of high school equivalency diplomas had lower GPAs than those who were traditional high school graduates (Klein and Grise 1987). In a further step, "GPA risk" was identified as a possible correlate of "attrition risk" (Jenkins et al. 1981), thus using a low GPA as a screening device for admitting students to a specially designed anti-attrition program.

Third, many of the new students also had different rates of progression as they moved through educational institutions. The State Higher Education Executive Officers (SHEEO) Association's task force on the achievement of minority students (1987) studied the rates of progression of minority and majority students over an 18-year period from fall 1968 to fall 1986; it found significant differences between the groups in the length and pattern of time required to complete a degree. Moreover, the freshman year's experience was found to correlate with slower rates of progression as well as attrition (Dumphy et al. 1987).

A fourth type of risk also differentiated the new students. For the most part, females, minorities, other disadvantaged students, and older adults had a lower probability of choosing a major in mathematics- and/or science-related areas. A comparison of the performance of males and females in engineering and science to determine whether gender correlated with attrition from those majors and with general persistence found positive correlations (Schoenberger 1988). Another study found that differences in overall GPA across groups may explain the differential performance in science courses (Sollimo 1988). Specifically, it found that attrition in chemistry at Burlington County College was highly correlated with an overall GPA of less than 2.0. Even in nursing, an area that has been historically female, the risk of "field attrition" actually increased during the seventies and early eighties as an increasing proportion of nursing students either dropped out or switched to a non-science-based major (Reed and Hudepohl 1983).

During the seventies, the described differences in the experiences of the new students and the more traditional students led analysts to apply a number of descriptive terms, "high-risk students," "disadvantaged students," and "poorly prepared students" but a few of them (Pruitt 1979; Spann

1977). Such terms were used to heighten the fact that the probability of an equal collegiate experience across class, gender, and racial/ethnic lines was—and is—myth rather than reality.

Characteristics of nontraditional students

Although characteristics of high-risk students sometimes correlated with those of nontraditional students, the two concepts had different denotations. One researcher defined new students or nontraditional students as being adults, students from lower socioeconomic levels, ethnic minorities, and women (Arfken 1981). A similar broad-based definition described adults, females, minorities, and, interestingly, students with below-average GPAs as nontraditional (Cohen and Brauer 1982), thus implicitly unifying the definitions of high risk and nontraditional.

A somewhat unusual perspective suggested that any group other than white, middle-income male students with average to greater-than-average high school records should be included in the label "nontraditional" (Radcliffe and Baxter 1984). Others included commuters and part-time students in their definitions of nontraditional students (Metzner and Blair 1987); still others reserved the term "nontraditional students" to denote adult enrollees (Cross 1979; Pinkston 1987). Given such confusion in definitions, it becomes important to ask when nontraditional students are also high risk.

Comparative analysis of nontraditional and high-risk students

Based on existing research, it is clear that the term "nontraditional student" merely refers to the changed student profile that emerged during the late sixties and early seventies as a consequence of demographic and sociopolitical change. In contrast, "high risk" is a theoretical concept based on an implicit assessment of the degree of negative risk associated with the educational experience. Thus, some nontraditional students are not high risk, and some high-risk students are traditional rather than nontraditional. Various combinations of nontraditional characteristics, however, appear to be at work to reduce the probability of equality of options as a consequence of the educational experience. For example, a student who is both older and academically underprepared could be considered both nontraditional and high risk (Pinkston 1987).

Similarly, an older minority student who commutes could experience a higher probability of adversities in attending college and become high risk (Sharkey et al. 1987). Adult females might also be high risk (Starks 1987).

Such interrelationships across the correlates of "nontraditional" can create risks in some students' educational experiences in the international as well as national arena. A study of students over 25 years old at the University of Sheffield, England, found a high correlation between older, nontraditional students and high-risk students (Roderich and Bell 1981). Interestingly, however, other researchers reported that older high-risk students participated more in the remediation program at the University of Massachusetts than did their younger counterparts (Noel 1978). Subsequently, these students had higher levels of persistence and higher GPAs than the younger students.

It is therefore important for administrators, counselors, professors, and other college personnel to understand that substantial differences may characterize nontraditional and high-risk students. Even among traditional students, the lowest one-third of the student population may be at risk (Noel 1978). Thus, programs must continue to be designed to address the special needs of such high-risk populations—which then raises a question: "Who are the high-risk populations?"

Demographic Characteristics of High-risk Students
Ultimately, risk as defined by complete withdrawal from the educational experience, or attrition, is the last phase in a broader network of such definitions. A declining or low GPA, failure to succeed in a chosen major, alienation from campus life, and financial problems are a few of the factors that may interact to cause a student's withdrawal. Additionally, more recent research indicates that a large element of attrition is unexplainable by these factors. That is, in some cases, no demographic, socioeconomic, or academic factors can be directly linked with the risk of not completing collegiate goals. An institutional follow-up of nonreturning students indicates that 85 percent of the sample felt that no intervention strategy could have altered their decision to leave the college (Cotnam and Ison 1988).

Other results could also be reinterpreted as indicative of this unexplained aspect of attrition (Heard 1988b). A follow-up study of nonreturning students at Shelby State Community College in Tennessee found that the interviewees themselves were confused about their decision to drop out. For instance, students in good academic standing cited "academic" factors as responsible for their decision to leave. Despite the specific explanatory variables employed and/or the specific type of attrition under discussion, some demographic groups, however, do appear more vulnerable than others.

Race/ethnicity

Evidence suggests that minority students have disproportionately higher risk of attrition and lower GPAs and are more undecided about their major field than majority students. The risk attached to African-American students, for example, extends backward to their elementary and secondary school experiences and forward to their graduate and professional school experiences (Clewell 1987).

A number of other studies have similarly identified African-Americans, Hispanics, and Native Americans as at risk in terms of attrition, GPA, and progression rates. Astin's now-classic study, for example, identified these racial/ethnic groups as prone to attrition (1975). Not surprisingly, the patterns of attrition Astin identified almost precisely followed the prevailing patterns of racial and ethnic social stratification. That is, white Americans had the lowest attrition rates, and African-Americans, Native Americans, and Hispanics had higher attrition rates.

A number of institutions have embarked on intervention programs to help high-risk students complete their studies. Northeastern University implemented intervention programs to reduce risk resulting from low GPA among African-Americans (Gordon 1987), and Miami-Dade Community College implemented a program with a similar aim for part-time African-American students (Belcher 1987). Based on interviews with students who dropped out of a historically black university, an action program was designed to retain enrolled students and to help nonreturning students adjust to their new status (Adams and Smith 1987).

Gender

In addition to race and ethnicity, gender is a demographic variable that has been associated with increased risk, but the results are mixed. It has been documented that females have a higher risk of attrition than males (Holahan et al. 1983), but another study found conflicting evidence (Illinois Community College Board 1987). The latter study, of trends in enrollment and program completion for 1984 to 1987, discovered that males were at higher risk for attrition than females. Or, put another way, a disproportionate number of females persevered. Field attrition was greater for females than males, however, with a greater proportion of males persisting in engineering technology and other "male" areas of concentration (see also Clagett and Diehl 1988).

To remedy the correlation between gender and field attrition, analysts have sought to untangle the causal variables that increase the risk associated with females in traditionally male fields. A number of sociocultural variables correlate with field risk among females (Ehrhart and Sandler 1987), including patterns of socialization, secondary school preparation and experiences, faculty attitudes, and parental attitudes. Another interesting finding regarding field risk among females is that when undergraduate females drop out of courses like chemistry and mathematics, they begin to question their intellectual capabilities (McDade 1988). In contrast, males see such moves as part of the process in a shift to a more "rewarding" field.

Athletes as high-risk students

While the demographic variables typically identified with high risk are race/ethnicity, gender, and age, others have been widely investigated. Less attention has been directed toward some other characteristics that do not fit neatly into existing categories.

Students who are athletes, for example, are often high risk both in terms of GPA and attrition (Ender 1983). A number of proposals have been made for reducing both types of risks by using new admissions criteria to screen out "less prepared" athletes. Recently, several propositions have been considered by the National Collegiate Athletic Association regarding higher SAT scores and higher grade point averages to reduce attrition and GPA risk among college athletes.

Nontraditional predictors of success—interest in athletics and other extracurricular activities, leadership ability, and so on—are predictors of academic achievement as powerful as traditional variables (such as SAT scores and academic record), however (Tom 1982). And in the long run, the nontraditional predictors are more accurate (Tom 1982). Thus, rather than increasing reliance on traditional predictors of academic success, one university permitted high-risk athletes to reduce course loads while improving skills through a self-paced course.

The finding that GPA and test scores may be less than satisfactory predictors of risk for athletes has been confirmed by other researchers working with other demographic groups. For example, when the Nelson-Denny reading test was used to predict risk among economically disadvantaged students of all races and ethnic backgrounds, the test scores proved to be more accurate for economically disadvantaged white students than for racial and ethnic minority students (Yamagishi and Gillmore 1980). Other findings, however, were contradictory (Nisbet 1982). Again, while such data indicate that risk is associated with athletes as an intracollegiate "demographic" group, additional research is needed before strategies can be designed to reduce risk in this population.

... GPA and test scores may be less than satisfactory predictors of risk for athletes...

Transfer students

Transfer students are another subgroup that may be disproportionately at risk. A study by the coordinating board of the Texas college and university system found a slightly higher persistence rate among nontransfers than among transfer students (see also Cuyahoga Community College 1987). Indeed, not only were transfer students somewhat less likely to graduate; they also had lower progression rates as a consequence of their transfer. In response, transfer students with GPAs below 2.0 at the University of Maryland in College Park were invited to participate in an intervention program (Boyd 1987).

Recognizing that transfer students may be at greater risk, Southwest Texas State University also established an intervention program. In 1976, approximately 39 percent of transfer students had GPAs of 3.00 or above on a 5.00 scale during their initial semester. By 1979, the percentage had increased to 62.9 percent, suggesting that the risk associated with transferring can be reduced.

International students

International students are another "demographic" group that has received little attention from researchers. In 1980, 312,000 nonimmigrant foreign students attended America's institutions of higher education. By 1987, that number had increased to 350,000, and the pattern of enrollment by country of origin had shifted dramatically (U.S. Dept. of Commerce 1989). In other words, a type of attrition had occurred. In 1982, for example, 20,000 Nigerian students were studying in this country. By 1987, the number had decreased to only 14,000—a 30 percent decrease. In contrast, the number of students from Asia, Europe, and Canada had increased. Latin America, like Africa, experienced a net loss in the number of students studying in this country (see table 4).

TABLE 4

FOREIGN (NONIMMIGRANT) STUDENT ENROLLMENT IN INSTITUTIONS OF HIGHER EDUCATION: 1982 AND 1987

	1982	1987	Percent Change
Africa	42,000	32,000	–23.8
Nigeria	20,000	14,000	–30.0
Asia	181,000	210,000	+16.0
Europe	29,000	36,000	+24.1
Latin America	55,000	43,000	–21.8
Canada	15,000	16,000	+ 6.7

Source: U.S. Dept. of Commerce 1989, table no. 255, p. 152.

Such changing patterns of international, nonimmigrant enrollment raise a number of macro-questions regarding causes. These patterns also suggest the need to give more attention to the micro-aspects of the issue, such as racism and the subsequent risk associated with international students on a campus. Some evidence suggests that international students may experience greater risk than noninternational students (Boyer and Sedlacek 1987). Environmental rather than individual factors have been identified as most relevant to the persistence of international students, another area where additional research is needed.

Demographic variables versus environmental variables
Demography is the study of the characteristics of various population groups. Environmental variables could indeed constitute a key intervening variable mediating demographic characteristics and risk. For example, hearing-impaired students on hearing campuses are high-risk students, but hearing-impaired students at postsecondary institutions for the hearing impaired might have lower attrition rates than non-hearing-

impaired students on hearing campuses (Scherer et al. 1987). Overall attrition rates are approximately one-third higher for hearing-impaired students than for hearing students, however (Scherer et al. 1987).

A study of attrition patterns at eight public and private colleges and universities found that, on average, majority students experience less risk of attrition than do minority students on majority campuses (Gosman et al. 1982). The converse occurs, however, when majority students matriculate at minority institutions. Some evidence also suggests lower attrition rates, higher progression rates, and lower field attrition rates for females who attend women's colleges. Thus, while demographic correlates of risk exist, these characteristics interact with a number of other variables.

Socioeconomic Characteristics of High-risk Students

In the American society, the demographic traits of race/ethnicity, gender, and age correspond to some degree with America's system of social stratification, but the system of social stratification operates beyond the boundaries of demography and creates socioeconomic and behavioral manifestations of the structural inequalities. Sociologists refer to this dimension as "patterned class behaviors." Indeed, it is through patterned class behaviors that a system of social stratification perpetuates itself. Thus, it becomes important to ask whether certain socioeconomic traits correlate with risk or whether certain socioeconomic variables operate to reduce the probability of educational success for historically disadvantaged students.

Socioeconomic status

Higher socioeconomic status provides numerous advantages in American society. People of higher socioeconomic status have, by definition, more income, higher education, and greater wealth as primary characteristics. Additionally, people of higher socioeconomic status have fewer divorces, enjoy a longer life expectancy, and report themselves to be happier than people of lower socioeconomic status (Collier and Smith 1982). Thus, it is less than surprising that a direct correlation exists between and among attrition, GPA, progression rate, field of study, and socioeconomic status.

A survey that was used to collect biographic information from high- and low-risk students to expand the correlates of risk beyond demographics found that males who persisted were characterized not only by strong academic backgrounds but also by higher socioeconomic status (Schaffer 1981). For female persisters, however, socioeconomic status was a less important predictor. Socioeconomic status, however, was also found to have a major effect on African-American students' persistence at white institutions.

Some evidence also exists that socioeconomic status may be a less important predictor of risk for African-Americans than other factors. A study of 80 academically underprepared African-American students at the University of Pittsburgh found that family background was not a statistically significant predictor of risk in this sample (Eddings 1982). Rather, "on-campus academic behavior"—carrying out assignments and completing homework—had the greatest explanatory power.

Many African-American students tend to experience higher risk because of their lower socioeconomic status. In 1979, median income for African-American families was $10,133 (U.S. Dept. of Commerce 1989). Yet of the African-Americans enrolled in a special admissions program at Livingstone College in 1979, more than 50 percent were from households with median incomes below $6,000, and 97 percent were from households with median incomes of $12,000 or less (Farrow 1980). During this same period, 54 percent of the participants in a program for both white and minority economically disadvantaged youth at Mansfield State College (Pennsylvania) came from families with a median parental income of less than $6,100 per year (Baylor 1982). Interestingly, none of the students in the program reported themselves as majoring in science or mathematics; education, business, and/or the social sciences were the chosen areas of concentration.

An extensive study of high-risk students in 58 different colleges and universities across the country defined two trends that summarize the relationship between socioeconomic status and risk (Coulson et al. 1981). First, the research indicated that students whose parents earned higher incomes experienced less risk of all types. In other words, they had higher rates of persistence, higher GPAs, and higher rates of progression. Second, similar patterns existed among students who received large amounts of financial aid and students who received more compensatory services. Other findings support Coulson's (Carroll 1987); a study of the relationship between financial aid and persistence found statistically significant levels of attrition between low-income students who received no grants and those who received grants that equaled at least

50 percent of tuition. These findings held for at-risk students in public universities, where even those students who received small grants persisted at higher rates than students of similar characteristics who received no grants.

An examination of more than 30 research studies addressing the relationship between financial aid and persistence reported that the presence of financial aid reduced risk among lower-income students to almost the same level that prevailed among middle- and upper-income students (Murdock 1987). Similarly, another study found that only a small positive relationship existed between financial aid and persistence (Moline 1987). The findings of these studies thus provide evidence that the risk associated with socioeconomic disadvantage can be ameliorated.

Parental education and occupation
While the economic variables associated with risk can be directly targeted, other socioeconomic factors as correlates of risk are less easily addressed. Family and family background, for example, are critical factors in the socialization and acculturation of the young, and it is possible that students can be socialized into patterns of behavior that increase risk. Although researchers have not identified socialization and acculturation as intervening links between risk and family background, a correlation does appear to exist. In one study, for example, a lower level of parental education correlated with a higher risk of attrition (Astin 1975). Other researchers found a relationship between parental education and GPA and risk of attrition (Lavin et al. 1983).

Another study further refined the relationship between parental education and risk (Skinner and Richardson 1988), separating minority persisters into groups based on parental education, students' academic preparedness, and motivation for a college degree. The study found higher levels of persistence in the academically prepared minority students whose parents were college graduates and who were committed to higher education. "Questioning the value of higher education" was more predictive of attrition than was level of parental education, however.

The Concept of High-risk Students: Problems and Limitations
The collegiate experience is replete with inequality of opportunities and outcomes. Elementary school students ex-

perience different levels of risk with regard to GPA and progression. High-risk students have different probabilities associated with the receipt of a high school diploma (Luxenberg 1977). If students do receive a diploma, those low-income students with high grades and high SAT scores have a lower probability of entering a prestigious university than their higher-income counterparts. Given the complexities of these problems, analysts have narrowed the focus of their research from the broader spectrum of educational inequalities to the more manageable issue of the differential risks of attrition characterizing different demographic and socioeconomic groups.

Some problems of theory and method have emerged from the wide array of research. First, problems have arisen in reaching consensus on the proper terminology to be used in addressing those students with the highest probability of not completing their educational program. Thus, "nontraditional," "high risk," "developmentally underprepared," "nonpersister," and other terms are all conceptual expressions that have been used to describe those groups at greater risk of low performance and attrition.

Second, even when risk of attrition has been identified as the problem area for educational institutions to target, it has been difficult to determine what should be included in the measurement construct. For example, some students are admitted but never register for class (Ross 1987). Should these numbers be included in measuring the rate of attrition? More important, should administrators and faculty create intervention programs targeted to these groups? Similarly, some students have goals not related to a degree (Gresty and Hunt 1981; Hodges 1988; Lee 1987). Should they be included in measurements of attrition?

Measuring the risk of attrition has also been affected by the lack of differentiation between freshmen and transfer students entering a college or university, as the two groups are often jointly included as part of an incoming class. Similarly, students leaving to transfer to another school have often been counted as nonpersisters (Fordyce 1988).

Third, as the conceptual focus has shifted from risk to attrition, the conceptual links between unequal educational opportunity and social stratification in the general society have been lost. The findings of a synthesis of research on dropping out of higher education suggest that for high-risk demographic groups like minorities and females, every aspect of educational attainment is highly correlated with social origin (Tinto 1975). In contrast, for "traditional" groups, such as whites and males, educational attainment is more directly the outcome of individual ability.

Given such conceptual shortcomings, the emphasis in this monograph is on risk and attrition. This explicit theme includes the various categories of risk accompanying specific groups in institutions of higher education. The implicit theme, however, reflects the broader risks that accompany sociocultural diversity in our society. The concept, profiles, and characteristics of a high-risk student can be fully understood only within this context.

THE IMPACT OF HIGH-RISK STUDENTS ON SOCIETY

The presence of differential rates of risk among students in higher education is not benign. Those students who persist receive private benefits that include financial and nonfinancial rewards. In 1987, for example, the mean annual income of persons having completed four years or more of college was $50,879. In contrast, the mean income of college dropouts, or those who had completed only one to three years of college, was $34,677 (U.S. Dept. of Commerce 1989, p. 442). Thus, the mean income of these nonpersisters was only 68 percent as high as that of persisters (see table 5).

TABLE 5

MEAN INCOME OF PERSISTERS AND NONPERSISTERS[a] BY RACE/ETHNICITY AND EDUCATION

Level of College Education	All Races	Whites	African-Americans	Hispanics
1–3 Years	$34,677	$35,646	$26,078	$31,367
4 Years	$50,879	$51,669	$37,700	$46,163

Ratios:
Nonpersisters (all races) to Persisters (all races) = .68
African-American Persisters to White Persisters = .73
African-American Persisters to White Nonpersisters = .95
Hispanic Persisters to White Persisters = .89

[a]"Persisters" refers to students who completed a four-year degree; "nonpersisters" refers to students who dropped out of college in under four years.

Source: U.S. Dept. of Commerce 1989, table no. 716, p. 442.

For minority groups, however, the payoff for persistence was substantially lower than for their majority counterparts. African-American persisters earned 73 percent as much as white persisters. Hispanic persisters had incomes 89 percent as high as white persisters. White nonpersisters, however, had incomes 95 percent as high as African-American persisters (see table 5). As would be expected, persisters of all racial and ethnic backgrounds earned more than their nonpersisting counterparts. Thus, attrition and risk are individually costly.

While data are available to document the importance of risk of attrition, little data exist on differences in economic circumstances that occur as a consequence of high or low GPAs. Substantial evidence documents the importance of "field attrition," however (Ehrhart and Sandler 1987; McDade 1988). That is, students who shift from science and mathematics and/or other more technical majors incur losses. In other words, they receive fewer financial rewards from obtaining a four-year degree. In 1988, the mean monthly salary offered to graduates with a bachelor's degree ranged from $2,119 for civil engineers to $2,237 for mathematics majors to $2,672 for petroleum engineers. Social science majors, however, were offered monthly salaries of only $1,881 (College Placement Council 1989).

Other gains may also accrue to those college students who persist and graduate. Private economic gains from completing a college degree extend beyond wages (Duncan 1976); that is, college graduates also have better working conditions and more comprehensive fringe benefits, and these additional benefits may also accrue by major. Thus, persisters do receive private benefits that nonpersisters must forgo.

The presence of risk for particular demographic and socioeconomic groups involves more than benefits forgone. Attrition, low GPAs, slow rates of progression, change from a more rigorous to a less rigorous major, and similar behaviors create direct costs for educational institutions and for the broader society.

The Effects of Attrition on Funding, Facilities Planning, and Long-term Academic Curricula

The impetus for reducing risk and attrition (broadly defined as the failure of an enrollee to meet his or her objectives for enrollment [Tinto 1975]) transcends the realm of altruism. College administrators are keenly aware of the economic burdens associated with risk and attrition. Indeed, it is institutions of higher education that must bear the direct financial costs of risk and attrition. The links are quite clear. Even today, full-time enrollments (FTEs) are critical to an institution's continued survival. High levels of attrition, even if the attrition is predictable, reduce FTEs and affect patterns of funding, facilities planning, and long-range planning for the curriculum (Gresty and Hunt 1981; Lenning, Beal, and Sauer 1980; Tinto 1975).

Patterns of funding

Patterns of funding are directly related to the level of FTEs. In 1987, 12.8 million students were enrolled in institutions of higher education (U.S. Dept. of Education 1989, p. 9). By 1997, the number of students enrolled in college is projected to increase slightly, to 13.0 million. The rate of increase of full-time students is lower than that of part-time students. In 1987, 7.23 million students were enrolled full time, 5.5 million part time. In 1997, the enrollment is projected to be 7.24 million full-time and 5.8 million part-time students (Gerald, Horn, and Hussar 1989, p. 28). Thus, funding is and will continue to be affected by both the number and the attendance status of the students who enroll.

As mentioned, attrition and risk disrupt patterns of funding. Declining enrollments, for example, leave unused building capacity. Disproportionately larger numbers of part-time or academically underprepared and/or low-income students increase average costs per student. When students enroll and do not complete their programs, such problems are magnified. And indeed, colleges' and universities' need for funding has increased at a rate far exceeding the rate of increase in student enrollments. Table 6 indicates that while aggregate enrollments in higher education increased by 11.2 percent from 1975 to 1980, current fund revenues for all institutions of higher education increased by 63.9 percent. From 1983 to 1986, the comparable rates of change were 0.6 percent for enrollment and 29.4 percent for funding.

TABLE 6

CURRENT REVENUES AND CHANGES IN HIGHER EDUCATION ENROLLMENT FOR SELECTED YEARS

	1975	1980	1983	1986
Current revenues, total higher education (millions)	$35,687	$58,520	$77,596	$100,439
Total enrollment (thousands)	10,880	12,097	12,320	12,402
Percent change in revenues	–	+63.9	+32.5	+29.4
Percent change in enrollment	–	+11.2	+ 1.8	+ 0.6

Source: U.S. Dept. of Commerce 1989, table nos. 257, 249, and 250, pp. 153, 149, and 150.

While part of the increased funding occurred in an effort to upgrade the quality of higher education in the country in general, part of the increase may reflect the impact of high-risk students. For example, the proportion of expenditures for higher education allocated for instructional purposes actually decreased, from 34 percent in 1975 to 31.8 percent in 1986 (U.S. Dept. of Education 1988). In contrast, the proportion of expenditures for student services, scholarships and fellowships, and academic support increased during this same period.

During academic year 1986–87, 45.5 percent of all undergraduate students received some form of financial assistance (U.S. Dept. of Education 1989, p. 284). The proportion was even higher for institutions with disproportionately high numbers of high-risk students. In private for-profit institutions, for example, 84 percent of students received some form of financial aid during this period (U.S. Dept. of Education 1989, p. 286). Thus, high levels of risk can complicate the total funding process and the funding needs of institutions of higher education.

Facilities planning

While attrition and risk interfere with funding for institutions, facilities planning is particularly affected. Facilities, unlike faculty and staff, are fairly fixed, with only upward flexibility. That is, once facilities have been expanded, the costs of reversing the decision are prohibitive. Yet increasing enrollments place institutions under pressure to increase space and other facilities. Subsequent declines in enrollment, attrition, and/or secular trends may then leave underused facilities.

Funding for buildings has already increased at a rate far greater than enrollment. From 1975 to 1983, for example, funding for building space increased by 50.9 percent, compared to an 11.4 percent increase in enrollment. From 1983 to 1986, building funds increased by 50.3 percent, while enrollment increased less than 0.6 percent (U.S. Dept. of Commerce 1989). Underused space is inefficient space. Such inefficiency can occur in a number of ways.

Attrition raises the average fixed costs for the educational institution. Costs for building space, because they are fixed, decline as average enrollment increases and vice versa. Thus, attrition contributes to higher educational costs. Second, students who persist but shift from one major to another may reduce the efficacy of strategic planning and lead to excess demand for some facilities and inadequate demand for others. Similarly, students who must repeat courses create additional problems for those administrators who manage building space. Thus, the failure of students to complete their degree programs represents inefficient use of scarce institutional resources (Tinto 1975).

The long-term academic curriculum

Perhaps the greatest institutional complexity created by high-risk students falls within the realm of the long-term academic curriculum. Experiments with strategies to reduce risk have indicated that populations at risk have special needs. Specifically, colleges and universities are sometimes required to supplement the academic curriculum with remedial courses (Denman 1983; Walleri 1987). Additionally, nonacademic courses designed to address the specific needs of high-risk students may also be required. The provision of additional courses and activities designed to improve academic excellence, however, is insufficient (Ellison et al. 1987). Instead, courses and activities to integrate high-risk students more fully into the collegiate community may also be required.

These suggestions bypass theory and highlight practice. Risk and attrition have required changes in curriculum to facilitate persistence among high-risk students. And they have been quite broad. Donnelly College in Kansas City, for example, expanded its curriculum to include specially developed courses in mathematics, English, and psychology for its high-risk students. While the mathematics and English courses were designed to strengthen academic skills, the psychology class was structured with the objective of enhancing the self-image of high-risk students (Joyce 1980).

The University of Minnesota similarly changed the curriculum to address the needs of high-risk students. Specifically, the university created several "pilot education packages" that included both curricular and noncurricular activities designed to increase retention rates among minorities (Moen 1980). In contrast, Shelby State Community College in Tennessee altered its curriculum to include special courses for *high school students*. The objective of the change was to improve the academic and overall preparedness of high-risk students before their actual enrollment in college (Heard 1988a). Institutions

Even scholars whose earlier research constituted intellectual advocacy on behalf of high-risk students are now suggesting retreat.

have changed curricula in numerous other ways, seeking to include such changes as part of their efforts to manage enrollment.

While some changes in curricula have been directly related to the efforts of colleges and universities to reduce attrition, other changes in curricula related to risk have been indirect. Moreover, most institutions of higher education include basic core courses that are required of all students, although a large part of the curriculum reflects the choices and preferences of students. Thus, students who change majors affect curriculum development. Or, academically underprepared students who choose majors that they perceive as less academically challenging affect curriculum development. That is, the institution may develop a reputation for its "soft" course offerings. Thus, even when high-risk students do persist and graduate, the long-term academic curriculum of institutions of higher education may be affected obliquely and nonlinearly. Accordingly, the pattern of change in undergraduate degrees conferred in 1971 and 1986 may reflect the special preferences of high-risk students as well as the preferences in curricula of students who are not high risk (McDade 1988; U.S. Dept. of Commerce 1989, p. 157).

Over recent years, some educational institutions have retreated from their initial level of involvement with high-risk students (Jaschik 1987). This retreat reflects, to a large extent, the basic curricular dilemma that plagues schools with large numbers of high-risk students. Basically, colleges and universities are faced with the choice of reducing the numbers of such undergraduates by changing admission standards, reducing the rigor of the curriculum, and/or changing the curriculum so that it enhances the educational development of high-risk populations, thereby permitting them to persist and graduate.

Even scholars whose earlier research constituted intellectual advocacy on behalf of high-risk students are now suggesting retreat. One previous advocate for high-risk students has suggested that community colleges reduce the numbers of high-risk students accepted and focus on improving the curriculum (Richardson 1983), subsequently advocating the use of "color-free" strategies at a time when the status of "colored" populations is so unfree as to make the term an oxymoron (Richardson and De Los Santos 1988). Such reactive responses are of course a consequence of the burdens imposed by high-risk students on institutions of higher education over the last decade. Continued "persistent" behavior on the part of institutions is necessary, requiring adequate levels of funding as well as creative strategies. Given the changing labor market, however, institutions of higher education are implicitly mandated to persevere and increase rather than decrease their commitment to high-risk students.

High-risk Students and the Future Labor Market

While the immediate impact of high-risk students is on the students and the institutions that serve them, the long-term impact falls, as mentioned, on society. To be more precise, the growth and productivity of the total economy can be constrained by the presence of a labor force that does not embody the levels of education and training needed for high levels of productivity. And, indeed, over the last few years, questions have been raised regarding the educational preparedness of the increasing numbers of females and minorities entering the workplace. The most casual review of business literature reveals titles like "Danger: Worker Shortage Ahead" and "Labor Scarcity: It's Costly and Will Get Worse" (Kovack 1986). Still other articles focus on the changing structure of the labor market (Kleinschrad 1987; Semerod 1987). Such research and data raise two major questions for both society and for institutions of higher education.

1. What will be the nature and structure of the labor force as America approaches the 21st century?
2. What role can institutions of higher education play in ensuring that the labor force is adequately trained?

While the essentially probabilistic nature of socioeconomic forecasting forbids precise responses to these queries, existing data can provide tentative answers to these questions.

Characteristics of the future labor force

Perhaps the most widely accepted source of projections for the labor market is the data generated by the Bureau of Labor Statistics (BLS) of the U.S. Department of Labor. The Bureau uses historical data to develop a set of socioeconomic assumptions that serve as the basis for annual forecasts of the labor market. The accuracy of the projections depends, of course, on the accuracy of the demographic, economic, political, sociological, and behavioral assumptions used as well as the accuracy of the statistics. Past assumptions, for example, have led to forecasts that were 1.7 to 2.9 percent below predicted levels (Fullerton 1982). In general, BLS's projections for the labor market are based on the assumption that continued growth in population will dictate growth in the labor market. Thus, the projections have focused less on the actual level of aggregate participation in the labor force and more on the size and structure of net additions to the labor supply.

While previous projections do not document a declining labor force, previous and current projections do indicate a slower rate of growth in the labor force in the nineties than in earlier decades. For example, projected growth in the labor force for the eighties was 16.4 percent, compared to 11.5 percent growth in the nineties. It is important to note, however, that recent projections have reestimated upward the size of the labor force. In 1985, for example, the labor force consisted of 115.5 million people. In 1980, BLS had projected a labor force in *1985* of 115 million, some 10 million more than its mid-1970 growth projections (104.4 million) (unpublished BLS tables, September 1987). The Bureau's more recent projections, using midyear assumptions regarding growth, project a labor force of 125 million in 1990 and 139 million people in 2000 (U.S. Dept. of Labor 1987). Thus, existing BLS research forecasts continued growth in the labor force. Why, then, do rumors of a labor shortage persist?

Two interactive factors support the thesis of an impending shortage. First, moderate projections of GNP predict an annual average growth rate of 2.4 percent (U.S. Dept. of Labor 1987), while the annual rate of growth in the labor force is projected at 1.2 percent. Second, the demographic composition of the labor force, like that of institutions of higher education, is changing. Only 10 percent of the growth in the labor force will consist of the demographic group that has been the traditional core of both the labor market and colleges and universities—white males.

The majority of the growth in the labor force will emerge from the same demographic groups who constitute high-risk students, that is, disadvantaged populations, African-Americans, Hispanics, females, and older people. Indeed, given the lower participation rate in the labor force of these groups as well as the higher rates of unemployment (with the exception of females), historically disadvantaged groups account for a potential source of even greater growth in the labor market.

Recent projections for the labor market indicate that 57 percent, or 11.9 million, of new entrants in the labor market will consist of racial and ethnic minorities (U.S. Dept. of Labor 1987). Such projections reflect the relatively higher birth and migration rates of these populations. The proportion of minority workers in the future work force could, as mentioned earlier, be further increased through measures designed to reduce unemployment among minorities and increase their participation in the labor force.

In October 1988, for example, the unemployment rate for African-Americans (10.8 percent) was 2.3 times that for whites (4.8 percent) (U.S. Dept. of Labor 1988). The unemployment rate for Hispanics (7.4 percent) was 1.5 times the rate for whites. Of equal concern, African-Americans were one-third of those potential participants in the labor market who had simply stopped looking for work because they believed that jobs were unavailable (U.S. Dept. of Labor 1988). Thus, behavioral as well as demographic factors indicate additional potential for growth in the labor market among racial and ethnic minorities.

Similarly, it is projected that females will constitute 47 percent of the *total* labor force in 2000 and 63 percent of the net growth in the labor force (U.S. Dept. of Labor 1988). Again, however, the potential exists for even greater participation by females. Currently, females make up 52 percent of the total population and 44 percent of the labor force. Colleges and universities will be called upon to assist in the preparation of some of these potential workers to prevent a shortage of skilled workers.

Institutions of higher education and the future labor market

These data pose a challenge to educators, administrators, and counselors. If institutions of higher education are to assist in preventing a shortage of labor, high-risk populations require services beyond the awarding of a degree. A new charge is mandated. Females, minorities, and other groups must persist in fields that provide the skills required for the occupational structure that will exist in 2000.

BLS's projections of employment are from three perspectives—fastest-growing jobs, fastest-declining jobs, and largest

job growth. While the fastest-growing occupations are projected to be in areas requiring higher education, the occupational areas with the largest job growth do not require a bachelor's degree (U.S. Dept. of Labor 1987). Approximately 27 percent of all projected jobs in 2000 will be in occupations requiring a bachelor's degree or higher, leaving approximately 73 percent that do not require a bachelor's degree. Thus, the role of two-year as well as four-year colleges may become even more critical.

The basic problem of an adequately trained work force, however, transcends the broad issue of secondary education versus higher education. Successful preparation for the labor market of the future instead requires that high school and college counselors and advisers become more aggressive in distributing information to students. What types of jobs will exist in 2000? How many jobs will be available in each area? What technical skills will be required in each job category? What types of attitudes and human relations skills are congruent with maximum productivity in each occupational area? Which jobs require skills of divergent thinking and which ones convergent thinking? What types of incentives will induce workers to choose low-paying, marginal jobs? To what degree will such jobs be automated? Such questions imply that advisers and counselors must function as "change agents" (Connell and Gardner 1982).

Current preparedness for the labor market
A number of studies have indicated that participants in the emerging labor market may be underprepared for the future labor market (Adams 1988; Mitchem 1982; U.S. Dept. of Labor 1987). More specifically, these researchers indicate that students in the United States in general may be deficient in the specific higher-order thinking skills that the new labor market will require. And such deficiencies are greater among female and minority populations.

Existing deficits in skills apply to more functional as well as to academic areas. For example, relatively unskilled workers are now required to use computers. Yet even among college populations, computer use is proportionately lower among minorities, females, and other potential high-risk groups. In 1984, 48 percent of male college students, compared to 40.9 percent of female college students, reported themselves as regular users of computers. Similarly, 45.3 percent of white college students, compared to 36.7 percent of African-American college students, used a computer. Finally, 41 percent of Hispanic college students, compared to 44.5 percent of non-Hispanic college students, used a computer. Surprisingly, however, more part-time enrollees than full-time enrollees used a computer (U.S. Dept. of Commerce 1989).

Lower rates of college enrollment as well as higher rates of attrition by some demographic groups are major factors threatening the preparedness of workers of the future. The preparedness of minority groups for the labor market is of particular concern. African-Americans are a case in point.

Between 1977 and 1986, the gap in college enrollment rates for African-Americans and whites increased. Specifically, although the number of African-American high school graduates aged 18 to 24 increased and the number of their white counterparts aged 18 to 24 decreased, the college participation rates increased for whites from 33 percent in 1976 to 34.1 percent in 1986. For African-Americans, enrollment rates dropped, from 33.4 percent in 1976 to 28.6 percent in 1986 (Wilson and Carter 1988).

Additionally, attrition rates for African-Americans are disproportionately high. If retention is broadly defined as the attainment of a bachelor's degree within six years, substantial differences exist between African-Americans and whites. In 1986, only 25.6 percent of African-Americans had received a B.A. degree after six years at a four-year institution. The comparable figure for whites was 48 percent (Wilson and Carter 1988). Figures for attrition at the graduate level are considerably higher. Stated differently, retention rates are 50 to 75 percent lower for African-Americans than for whites (Educational Testing Service 1988).

Attrition, risk, and international competitiveness
The indirect impact of attrition and risk extends beyond the labor force to still another area. The U.S. economy is in general less competitive than in the past, and the challengers to America's competitiveness include not only Japan and other industrial countries like Great Britain and France but also developing countries like Brazil and India. Technological stagnation, decreased productivity, and inefficient capital markets are but a few of the factors that have contributed to the weakening of the United States in the global economy (Watson and Rowe *in press*).

A critical historical and contemporary factor in the growth of the United States has been the education and training of its labor force. Thus, it is not surprising that those challengers to America's historic position as a world economic power are also, for the most part, characterized by superior academic performance among students of higher education. If the needs of high-risk students are not addressed, America's international competitiveness may be further threatened as the next century approaches.

Conclusions and Implications

It is often said that education is a social good with benefits accruing to the broader society. The converse is also true. The opportunity costs associated with risk and attrition ultimately reduce the growth, development, and potential accomplishments of the broader society. Thus, it is critical that existing successful strategies be continued and new strategies be adopted to reduce attrition and to neutralize risk. Evaluation and discussion of strategies, however, require greater insight into the causal variables associated with this phenomenon. The next two sections examine both academic and nonacademic variables associated with risk and attrition.

ACADEMIC AND RELATED FACTORS ASSOCIATED WITH RISK AND ATTRITION

Risk and attrition are outcomes of a variety of interdependent variables—parental background and education, socioeconomic status, the degree of cognitive stimulation and preparation provided at home and school early in the developmental cycle, physical and mental health, and racism and discrimination, for example. High-risk students are typically at the lower end of the scale (or the negative side) for each variable. While a lengthy discussion is possible for each of these variables, for purposes of this monograph, the discussion is limited to academic and related factors.

America's educational institutions are failing to educate many students, particularly minorities, females, and other students from disadvantaged backgrounds. This failure begins in elementary school and continues throughout the educational pipeline to colleges and universities (Jones 1987). For many students, the negative effects are felt before kindergarten, because many high-risk students do not attend nursery school. For those who do receive some form of exposure before kindergarten, the instructional content and quality are often less enriching than those provided for students of higher socioeconomic status.

One failure of the system comes from not providing adequate funding and facilities for preschool programs for high-risk students. Head Start, for example, is a program that has proven beneficial to high-risk students. It was designed to provide compensatory education and child development services to low-income families. From its inception in 1965 to 1987, Head Start had saved approximately 10.5 million children (Jones 1988). Yet this number is only a fraction (16 percent in 1987) of the disadvantaged children who needed its services. Hence, many high-risk children begin their public school experience in kindergarten with the odds already stacked heavily against them. Further evidence of the system's failure to educate high-risk students can be seen by the high rates of attrition and by the wide gap in achievement that exist between low-risk and high-risk populations (Applebee, Langer, and Mullis 1989; Jones 1989a).

This section therefore addresses some major academic issues for primary and secondary schools as well as for colleges and universities. Successful resolution of these issues can result in gains for high-risk students in the 1990s and particularly by 2000. Specifically, it discusses three major issues:

poor academic background and preparation, inefficient instructional approaches used by teachers, and failure of teachers, administrators, and counselors to teach functional study habits and skills to these students. Precise processes by which systemic forces function to reduce the probability of academic achievement for high-risk students are discussed in the next section.

Academic Background and Preparation
High degrees of risk are differentially attached to some demographic and socioeconomic groups. These levels of risk, however, are not osmotically conferred. While American students have in general lost their competitive edge and are lagging behind students in other industrialized countries (U.S. Dept. of Education 1989), America's racial/ethnic and low-income groups are disproportionately worse off. Differential effort expended on students and their discriminatory treatment, in combination with factors specific to the student, interact to produce academic underpreparedness.

Preparation in schools: Differential access to knowledge
A number of factors affect what is taught in school and are therefore directly related to what and how students learn. American schools and colleges are not value-free institutions that merely provide knowledge (Kuh and Whitt 1988; Reyes and Stanic 1985). Rather, colleges and universities are social communities as well as educational institutions (Kuh and Whitt 1988), thus mirroring and perpetuating societal inequalities (Reyes and Stanic 1985). It is primarily in schools that students learn about sexual stereotypes and racial bias. Moreover, students of high socioeconomic status engage in more complex problem solving and exercises in authority, thus learning how to be leaders, while their counterparts of low socioeconomic status do repetitive drills and learn how to be followers. Further, the school curriculum seems to benefit certain groups (white male students of high socioeconomic status) more than other groups (African-American students, female students, and students of low socioeconomic status [Reyes and Stanic 1985]). While minority children often begin school with positive attitudes toward the institution, differences in race, gender, and social class begin to emerge during elementary school and increase by high school and college

(Beane 1985; Campbell 1986; Jones, Burton, and Davenport 1984; Reyes and Stanic 1985).[2]

Class, racial, sexual, and even cultural discrimination influence the quality and quantity of material taught in schools. Many low-income and minority youths, for example, attend overcrowded inner-city schools where the tax base is low and expenditures for education subsequently lower. Moreover, public schools' expenditures per pupil are greatly influenced by the revenue received from federal, state, and local governments as well as revenue received from taxes (U.S. Dept. of Education 1989, p. 148).

Even within states, patterns of inequitable and insufficient financing serve to undermine the ability of many communities to support their schools. Some school districts are able to spend two or three times as much money on their children's education as neighboring districts. In Massachusetts in 1982, for example, the annual expenditure per pupil varied from a high of $5,013 in Rowe to a low of $1,637 in Athol. Similarly, the top 100 school districts in Texas spent an average of $5,500 per child, compared with $1,800 spent by the bottom 100 school districts (National Coalition 1985).

The problem of financial inequity among educational institutions is complicated by other factors. Schools in the poorest districts face the double jeopardy of having students who are most at risk and the least amount of money to implement needed programs to improve the quality of education. Moreover, schools in some urban areas face additional costs because old buildings need constant repair and special security measures have to be implemented. Thus, the actual expenditure per pupil is further reduced and preparation is hindered by differential access to academic resources.

The relationship between academic underpreparedness of high-risk students and administrative decision making

Few social gatherings of middle-income minority parents occur without the recounting of horror stories regarding what has come to be called "tracking" (that is, placing students in groups according to perceived ability). The practice of tracking occurs widely at the primary and secondary levels, and

... low-achieving white, middle class students tend to be placed in higher tracks or ability groups.

---

2. See National Coalition 1985 for a more complete discussion of the effects of discrimination and differential treatment in children.

colleges and universities indirectly apply it. Because administrators rely on test results that many view as culturally biased together with the often subjective recommendations of teachers, certain demographic/socioeconomic groups may be disproportionately placed in lower tracks. Thus, they enter college at greater risk.

For example, African-American students are disproportionately found in classes for lower-ability groups or track levels. Even high-achieving African-American students tend to be placed in low-ability groups or tracks, while low-achieving white, middle-class students tend to be placed in higher tracks or ability groups (Raze 1984).

In some subject areas, deficiencies in preparation are difficult to repair. For example, early academic training is vital for the increased participation and performance of high-risk students in science and mathematics. Even more critical is that entry into these fields is made almost exclusively through appropriate educational training. Mathematics, a sequential subject, should be introduced in an atmosphere that fosters positive attitudes in students, enabling them to benefit to the utmost from the learning experience. Yet some teachers may transmit the attitude that achievement in mathematics is beyond the capability of high-risk students, thereby creating negative attitudes among those students.

While concerted efforts have been made nationally to educate American youth in mathematics and the sciences (American Association 1984), African-Americans and other minority high school students continue to be underrepresented in academic programs and overrepresented in vocational programs (College Entrance Examination Board 1985). An important implication of this distribution for educational achievement is that students in vocational education earn fewer school credits in areas like English, mathematics, and science. Moreover, the content of their courses in those academic subjects is often different from that in other curricular tracks. For example, they might take general mathematics rather than algebra and trigonometry or general science rather than biology and chemistry (College Entrance Examination Board 1985).

A study of high school seniors indicates that while 68 percent of African-American high school seniors took algebra I, a mere 39 percent took algebra II. The percentages of white high school seniors taking algebra I and II, however, were 81 percent and 51 percent, respectively. For Hispanic students, the rates were 67 percent and 38 percent, respectively (U.S. Dept. of Education 1981).

The percentages of all students taking trigonometry and calculus were much lower. For African-Americans, for example, they were 15 percent and 5 percent, respectively; for Hispanic students, 15 percent and 4 percent, respectively; and for white students, 27 percent and 8 percent, respectively. Similarly low percentages of students took science courses in 1980. The percentages of all African-American students enrolled in physics and chemistry classes in 1980 were 19 percent and 28 percent, respectively; of Hispanic students, 15 percent and 26 percent, respectively; and of white students, 20 percent and 39 percent, respectively (U.S. Dept. of Education 1981).

Other researchers have noted similar differences in academic preparation. A study of 42 high schools in 36 districts found that African-American students made up over half of the sample but that only one-third of them were enrolled in algebra II and another one-fourth in calculus (Marrett 1981). Further, a greater concentration of African-American students was enrolled in lower-level mathematics courses. Compared with one-quarter of the white students, nearly one-half of the African-Americans were in such courses. Furthermore, African-American students represented a slightly smaller percentage of all mathematics enrollees than they did of the total student population.

The literature indicates that an interactive relationship exists between academic background and academic performance. That is, a strong positive relationship exists between courses taken and achievement. The more mathematics studied by minority students, the better will be their performance on achievement tests (Jones, Burton, and Davenport 1984). And as test scores improve, so do the students' academic self-image (Olstad et al. 1981) and academic performance.

A comparison of the number of mathematics courses taken by African-American students and white students and their achievement in mathematics found, in addition to the expected correlations, that the number of mathematics courses taken helped to explain the differential achievement of African-American and white students in mathematics (Jones, Burton, and Davenport 1984). The percentage of African-American students taking only one course in mathematics was 37 percent, while it was 24 percent for white students. By comparison, 13 percent of African-American students but 31 percent of white students took three courses in mathematics (Jones, Burton, and Davenport 1984).

An analysis of the Third National Assessment of Educational Progress (NAEP III) in mathematics shows a substantial increase in achievement in mathematics for both African-Americans and whites with each mathematics course taken (Matthews et al. 1984). African-American students made greater gains than their white counterparts since the second mathematics assessment (NAEP II) in 1978, especially in exercises assessing knowledge and skill. They continued to score below the national level of performance, however.

In addition, African-American students in schools with large minority enrollments made greater than average gains, a positive step in the right direction arguing for the continuation of efforts to encourage minority students to enroll in advanced mathematics classes (Matthews et al. 1984). While test scores for minority students and females in mathematics and the sciences have been lower than the test scores for white males, the performance of minority students has improved significantly when they participate in compensatory programs (American Association 1984). These findings are also relevant for academic areas other than mathematics and science.

As one reviews the literature on academic background and preparation, it becomes clear that a number of systemic factors interact to create different degrees of academic underpreparedness among various demographic and socioeconomic groups. Even within the classroom, such practices continue to create underpreparedness.

Teachers' Inefficient Instructional Approaches
Teachers may be a child's most valuable resource after his or her parents. Indeed, many of a child's waking hours are spent with teachers. When a group of teenagers were asked "who or what influenced them to become the kinds of people they are, 58 percent mentioned one teacher or more. . . , 90 percent mentioned their parents, and 88 percent mentioned peers" (Csikszentmihalyi and McCormack 1986, p. 417). The evidence suggests, however, that teachers themselves may be a cause of academic underpreparedness and therefore of attrition and risk. For example, while 58 percent of students mentioned a teacher as a significant factor, the same students indicated that only 9 percent of all the teachers they had ever

encountered in the course of their school careers had made a difference in their lives. That is, *91 percent* of their teachers left no memorable mark.

These students indicated further that their classes were dull and boring and that school was one of the least favorite places they wished to be. Moreover, their favorite places in school were the cafeteria, the library, or the hallway (Csikszentmihalyi and McCormack 1986). In other words, for some students, the experience at school itself may lead to attrition, either actively or as a form of coping behavior. Strategies of emotion-focused passive coping often lead to avoidance behavior, that is, dropping out.

Do teachers intentionally contribute to attrition and risk, or are they not knowledgeable about differences among cultures? Have instructional techniques atrophied, causing teachers to disserve rather than to serve specific demographic or socioeconomic groups? Do males and females and/or racially or ethnically diverse groups exhibit differences in cognitive or information-processing style? And are some teachers unable and/or unwilling to vary their instructional style?

The relationship between information processing and cognitive development

A special relationship exists between students' styles of processing information and their level of cognitive development. Both information processing (i.e., how knowledge is organized in the mind and memory for later use) and cognitive development (i.e., how knowledge is carried and represented) are germane to the acquisition of higher-order skills (Driscoll 1982; Klausmeier and Associates 1979). The constructs of concrete reality and abstract concepts in the theory of information processing can be compared to the concrete and formal operations stages of Piagetian cognitive development theory.

According to Piaget's hypothesis, the thought processes of children between the ages of about six and 12 to 14 operate on a concrete, holistic level and require a great deal of visual-spatial stimulation. Piaget's next level of cognitive development, the formal operations stage, which children typically enter at about age 12 to 14, is characterized by the ability for abstract and analytical thinking (Driscoll 1982).

The notion of holistic processing in the theory of information processing is characterized by a dependence on concrete

reality (akin to Piaget's concrete operations stage). On the other hand, analytic or more abstract processing is characterized by reasoning ability and higher-order thinking skills, similar to Piaget's formal operations stage of cognitive development (Wagner 1977).

Research has shown that some high school students never develop significantly beyond the concrete operations stage (Fennema and Behr 1980; Klausmeier and Associates 1979). This case seems to be true for high-risk students, many of whom fail to get the appropriate stimulation and learning experiences that would facilitate their advancement from a concrete to a more formal and analytic level of thinking and processing information. Without access to this type of reasoning ability, it is unlikely that these students will become high achievers in subjects like mathematics that require abstract reasoning. Children's development must be stimulated through intellectual challenge in higher-order skills to speed up the transitional period between concrete and formal thought (Klausmeier and Associates 1979).

Thus, it may well be that students' status as high risk in terms of academic achievement is more a function of their lack of exposure in the classroom to abstract and analytical reasoning processes than of inherent psycho-operational competencies. For example, it has been shown that instructional procedures emphasizing thinking aloud enabled students to construct hypothetical problems, analyze problems, and work through errors rather than avoid them (Fuller 1978; Resnick 1986). Thinking aloud enables a student's performance to be critiqued and shaped by peers or instructors—a process that cannot be done effectively when the results are all that are available, instead of the thought processes that go into arriving at a solution (Resnick 1986).

Such successful approaches to problem solving need to be developed for high-risk students. Prospective teachers in methods classes in teacher education programs must be sensitized to the special relationship that exists between students' styles of processing information and their level of cognitive development. Those teachers who are already in the classroom must be given in-service training. Teachers must be aware of the value of classroom learning experiences and the role they play in helping students move from a concrete, holistic style of processing to a more abstract and analytic mode.

Differences in styles of processing information

Students' cognitive factors are related to the acquisition of information and the development of thinking skills. Thus, an understanding of how different students process information and the strategies they use to solve problems can provide greater insight into attrition and risk. Those responsible for educating high-risk students must understand how they develop intellectually.

The research suggests that students' "good" and "poor" performance in abstract conceptual skills may be linked to development of abstract and concrete tendencies in processing information (Carpenter 1980; Driscoll 1982; Klausmeier and Associates 1979). Piaget's cognitive development theory explains that abstract thinking is associated with formal operational thought that in turn facilitates greater readiness for abstract concepts and complex problem solving (Wagner 1977).

Minorities' style of processing information has been found to be more concrete and perceptually dependent (holistic) (Shade 1984). Moreover, the cognitive development of many of these students appears to be arrested at the concrete operations stage because their *learning experiences* may have failed to develop their analytic capabilities beyond routine levels (Klausmeier and Associates 1979; Wagner 1977). Consequently, large numbers of these students are tracked into lower-level courses (Raze 1984).

To compensate for this apparent preferential style of processing some groups of students use, some researchers have suggested a differential instructional approach for students demonstrating a predominance in holism so as to challenge and evoke responses from their preferred domain (Olstad et al. 1981), although such a suggestion has the potential to systematically underchallenge the analytic capabilities of those students (Roberts 1990). A more useful approach may be to counter holistic, dependent tendencies with instructional approaches that help high school students overcome a dependency on a perceptually concrete learning mode and focus more on the formal operations consistent with their stage of cognitive development (Driscoll 1982).

Theory of information processing asserts that the cognitive styles of students with more conceptually developed cognitive structures facilitate more reliance on formal and abstract reasoning for working out the hypothetical systematically and less on perception and concrete reality (Fennema and Behr 1980; Wagner 1977; Witkin et al. 1977). "Information-processing style" has been defined as a continuum of cognitive styles associated with right-brain/left-brain functions (Fennema and Behr 1980); that is, each cognitive style represents two opposing extremes, such as impulsivity and reflectivity or field dependent and field independent (Fennema and Behr 1980).

At the one extreme, impulsive individuals have a tendency to act spontaneously, giving the first answers that come to mind. At the other extreme, reflective individuals tend to take time to explore the plausible alternatives to respond to questions and resolve problems (Fennema and Behr 1980). Field-dependent individuals tend to depend on global perception and demonstrate a need for an "inordinate" amount of concrete referents to work through problems (actual objects, pictures, graphs, diagrams, and so on) (Fennema and Behr 1980). Further, they tend to be holistic and focus on the total environment, giving credit to external referents and taking other people's views into account (Witkin et al. 1977). Conversely, field-independent individuals are analytical and perceive the environment in its components (Fennema and Behr 1980). Field-independent persons tend to rely on internal referents in a self-consistent way. Thus, they can quickly and efficiently extract important information from distracting influences (Witkin et al. 1977). Field-independence has been associated with many cognitive problem-solving skills necessary for manipulating and restructuring the world through symbolic thought processes. Moreover, these problem-solving skills correlate with existing instructional styles.

Field-dependent students could be at a disadvantage. They might, for example, need more visual or oral instructions in solving problems or definitions of performance outcomes than field-independent students. Moreover, relatively field-dependent students are not likely to do as well in mathematics and science as more field-independent students, given the way these disciplines are taught (Witkin et al. 1977).

Women and most racial minorities also think less analytically than white males, which is responsible for their lower academic performance in mathematics and science, and females and most racial minorities develop a more global and relational, less analytical, mode of processing information (Dunteman et al. 1979). Others challenge these conclusions, however (Prom 1982; Roberts 1990). Perhaps the instrumentation used for measuring the analytic mode, rather than the type of thinking itself, is a major factor in the observed difference (Prom 1982).

A paradigm of information processing, based on some groups' having developed a special cultural pattern and a specific method for organizing and processing information, illustrates the way that African-Americans perceive, encode, represent, and analyze information (Shade 1984). While the preferred modality for receiving information in the American culture is visual, the emphasis among African-Americans is on the kinetic and tactile senses. Moreover, African-Americans' cue selection is also different from that used by the majority culture (Shade 1984). (The selection of cues is important for encoding and representing information that will be retained from the barrage of information to which one is exposed.) Because, as the literature suggests, African-Americans are socialized to be person-oriented rather than object/thing-oriented (Prom 1982; Shade 1984), their cue-selection preferences tend to be people and events rather than ideas and objects. Contemporary instructional techniques, however, are based upon ideas and objects.

Minorities' and women's orientation toward people may be the result of the interaction between a variety of cultural and personal forces and the physical environment (Johnson and Prom 1984). It is this orientation that gives them a value orientation focused on people, which in turn predisposes them to careers in the social sciences and away from the natural and physical sciences and engineering.

Like the processing styles of impulsivity and reflectivity, however, field dependence and field independence are not mutually exclusive within any one person and should therefore not be considered an absolute dichotomy (Witkin and Goodenough 1981). Further, mutualism between the processing systems provides the individual with an increased level of intellectual strength (Kaufmann 1979). This point of view should provide the impetus for change for those who advocate holism as a fixed mode of learning to the exclusion of learning experiences in the classroom.

Thus, an important question is raised: Is holistic perception characteristic of minorities and women, or is holism tied to the lack of stimulation of latent analytic capabilities in these students?

. . . females and most racial minorities develop a more global and relational, less analytical, mode of processing information.

The effect of information-processing styles on learning for high-risk students

Psychoeducational studies agree that preferences of modality associated with holism in processing behavior should not be treated as "inferior" (Kaufmann 1979; Madhere 1989; Roberts 1990; Witkin et al. 1977). Instead, this processing style should be complemented with classroom and other learning experiences designed to challenge and stimulate more analytic thinking skills.

Most research on modality preferences of people of African heritage to date has failed to go beyond affective characteristics and patterns of socialization, thus providing an incomplete assessment of the functioning of their intellect (Madhere 1989). A structural model of the human mind, the "Three-Diamond Model of the Intellect," provides a comprehensive framework for objectively analyzing the functioning of the "black mind" (Madhere 1989). The model uses a combinative-systems paradigm to illustrate that an individual's capacity to combine processes makes the human mind versatile, suggesting that individuals' preferences for modality can be altered to stimulate and challenge thinking and learning (see figure 1).

Figure 1. The Three-Diamond Model of the Intellect

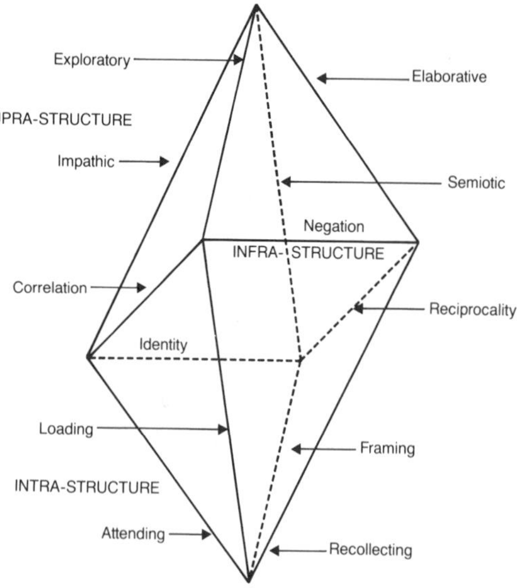

Taken From: Madhere, S. 1989. Models of Intelligence and the Black Intellect. *Journal of Negro Education* 58: 189–202.

The intellect is a combinative structure integrating three subsystems: an infrastructure, an intrastructure, and a suprastructure (Madhere 1989). The infrastructure involves the processes of attending, recollecting, loading, and framing. The intrastructure is characterized by the logical operations of identity, negation, correlation, and reciprocality. The suprastructure is comprised of processes that facilitate the formation of images, codes or symbols, concepts or constructs, and feelings and personal interactions. Thus, while the three subsystems function similarly in all humans, the suprastructure, more than the others, is culturally dependent, as it uses processes involving imagery, symbols, and constructs that obviously vary with the social and environmental milieu to which an individual is exposed.

In contrast to the numerous studies that report holism in African-Americans and other high-risk groups, empirical evidence suggests analytical tendencies among some African-American students. Studies with African-American students, however, support the conclusions of previous research on differences in achievement between students who demonstrate an abstract learning style and those who are concrete learners. That is, African-American students who had a reflective processing style and engaged in abstract reasoning earned higher grades than their counterparts who were classified as concrete learners (Bell 1974; Jones 1985; Vance and Engin 1978). Indeed, African-American students who were high achievers in mathematics were found to have profiles similar to higher-achieving students of other ethnic groups on important variables, such as problem solving, achievement in reading, IQ, socioeconomic status, achievement in mathematics, and mathematics self-concept (Bell 1974; Jones 1985).

A more recent study attempted to identify relationships among mode of processing behavior, level of cognitive development, and achievement in mathematics in a sample of urban African-American high school students (Roberts 1990). Only a modest amount of holism was found in the sample (32 percent), compared to what would be expected given the preponderance of literature that labels African-Americans as holistic. Just under half (46 percent) of the students used an integrated mode of processing behavior. Almost one-fourth of the sample (22 percent) were analytic, and they had higher scores in mathematics than both the integrated and the holistic students (Roberts 1990), underscoring the current liter-

ature that analytic processing behavior is hierarchically more germane to high school mathematics than holism.

It cannot be emphasized enough that holism should not be treated as inherent in African-Americans or other high-risk students, because doing so would prove to be systematically underchallenging for these students. Students who were taught by teachers who emphasized abstract reasoning had higher mean scores on national norm-referenced measures than students who were taught by teachers who focused on computation (Roberts 1989).

Instructional styles in the classroom

Because teachers are schooled to expect certain patterns of behavior and learning styles among different groups of students, they tend to vary their instructional styles. Even within a single classroom, instructors may use a different instructional style with different racial/ethnic and socioeconomic groups. As stated previously, schools tend to separate students according to differences in social class and racial group, so that minority and poor children are placed in lower tracks, taught more by rote and repetition, and discouraged from asking questions or participating in intellectual discourse. At the same time, white students and others of high social class are placed in the higher tracks, where questioning and discussion are encouraged (Resnick 1986).

Research has shown that teaching higher-order skills is critical to developing problem-solving abilities, an important prerequisite for academic success. Students of the more privileged social class are usually the chief beneficiaries of this type of instruction. Further, a historical look at educational institutions shows that higher-order goals have consistently been aimed at the elite. Mass education, on the other hand, has been largely concerned with developing routine abilities.

While schools today are not rigidly and centrally controlled, prevailing social conditions often limit the poor in terms of the degree to which they are allowed to attain these higher-order skills. It has been argued that the attainment of these higher-order concepts (through a focus on instruction demonstrating the interconnectedness of ideas, concepts, and relationships) is the key to academic success on an advanced level (Romberg and Tufte 1986). This situation is particularly true in some academic areas. It is widely recognized that a direct relationship exists between the amount and quality of educational experience (greatly influenced by socioeconomic class) and proficiency in higher-order problem solving (Resnick 1986).

Academic Underpreparedness: The Product of Multiple Interactive Causes

Lower socioeconomic status, a total world view that implicitly designates minority groups as "inferior," culturally biased testing tools, institutional practices like tracking, inappropriate teaching techniques, and similar variables *interactively,* not additively, produce greater risk for minorities and the disadvantaged. Yet analysts frequently cite data on the educational gap between various groups without putting the data in context. Indeed, as one reviews data on the numerous operative systemic forces, it is surprising that the gap in academic achievement is not greater.

This gap in achievement culminates in greater risk and attrition in institutions of higher education. African-Americans can be cited as a case in point. On surveys of reading proficiency conducted by the National Assessment of Educational Progress and administered by the Educational Testing Service (ETS), the reading proficiency score for 13-year-old African-Americans in 1983–84 was only slightly higher than the score for 9-year-old white students. The score for 17-year-old African-Americans was 0.2 less than the score for 13-year-old white students and 31.1 less than their 17-year-old white peers. Further, whereas 85 percent of white 17-year-olds had an intermediate proficiency level in reading, only 41.1 percent of their African-American peers were at that level in 1970–71. By 1983–84, the gap had narrowed, with African-American 17-year-olds scoring 65.8 percent and whites scoring 88.9 percent (U.S. Dept. of Education 1988) (see table 7).

In 1984, the writing performance of African-American 11th graders was lower than that of white 8th graders on NAEP's assessments of writing. Across all grade levels, however, the writing performance score for African-Americans was almost the same as the scores for students who resided in disadvantaged urban communities (U.S. Dept. of Education 1988) (see table 8).

In like manner, on NAEP's assessment of mathematics, African-American 9-, 13-, and 17-year-olds scored almost the same as students who lived in disadvantaged urban communities but much less than students from advantaged urban

TABLE 7

**GAP BETWEEN AFRICAN-AMERICANS AND WHITES
IN READING PROFICIENCY FOR AGES 9, 13, AND 17:
1974-75 AND 1983-84**

Age	Gap 1974-75	Gap 1983-84
9-Year-Olds	–34.0	–31.7
13-Year-Olds	–36.5	–26.6
17-Year-Olds	–46.7	–31.1

Note: Scores on the NAEP Reading Proficiency Test were evaluated at performance levels "adept," "intermediate," and "basic."

Source: U.S. Dept. of Education 1988, table no. 81, p. 102.

TABLE 8

**WRITING PERFORMANCE OF 4TH, 8TH, AND 11TH
GRADERS BY SELECTED CHARACTERISTICS
OF STUDENTS: 1984**

Selected Characteristics of Students	Grade 4	Grade 8	Grade 11
All Students	158	205	219
Sex			
Female	166	214	229
Male	150	196	209
Race			
African-American	138	186	200
White	163	211	224
Type of Community			
Rural	153	203	213
Disadvantaged urban	142	188	201
Advantaged urban	170	221	228

Note: The writing scale score ranges from 0 to 400 and is defined as the average of a respondent's estimated scores on 10 specific writing tasks. The average response is used to estimate average writing achievement for each participant as if each had performed all 10 writing tasks.

Source: U.S. Dept. of Education 1988, table no. 84, p. 105.

communities and whites (see table 9). On NAEP's assessment of science proficiency over the period from 1970 to 1986, African-American 9- and 13-year-olds increased their proficiency in science, whereas the proficiency among African-American 17-year-olds and whites at all three levels declined.

Nevertheless, over all three age levels, white students out-performed African-Americans (Mullis and Jenkins 1988) (see table 10).

TABLE 9

NATIONAL ASSESSMENT OF EDUCATIONAL PROGRESS IN MATHEMATICS FOR AGES 9, 13, AND 17 BY SELECTED CHARACTERISTICS OF PARTICIPANTS: 1981-82

Selected Characteristics of Students	Age 9	Age 13	Age 17
All Students	56.4	60.5	60.2
Sex			
Male	55.8	60.4	61.6
Female	56.9	60.6	58.9
Race			
African-American	45.2	48.2	45.0
White	58.8	63.1	63.1
Type of Community			
Rural	52.7	56.3	57.0
Disadvantaged urban	45.5	49.3	47.7
Advantaged urban	66.3	70.7	69.7

Source: U.S. Dept. of Education 1988, table no. 86, p. 106.

TABLE 10

TRENDS IN AVERAGE SCIENCE PROFICIENCY BY RACE: 1970 TO 1986

Race	Age 9		Age 13		Age 17	
	1970	1986	1970	1986	1970	1986
African-American	178.7	196.2	214.9	221.6	257.8	252.8
White	235.9	231.9	264.4	259.2	311.8	297.5

Source: Mullis and Jenkins 1988, pp. 28–29.

The trend continues for those African-American students who prepare to enter college. On the Scholastic Aptitude Test, African-American students scored about 100 points below whites on the verbal and mathematical portions from 1975–76 to 1986–87 (U.S. Dept. of Education 1988) (see table 11).

TABLE 11

SAT SCORE AVERAGES BY SEX AND RACE: 1975-76, 1980-81, AND 1986-87

	1975-76	1980-81	1986-87
SAT-Verbal,			
All Students	431	424	430
Sex			
Male	433	430	435
Female	430	418	425
Race			
African-American	332	332	351
White	451	442	447
SAT-Mathematical,			
All Students	472	466	476
Sex			
Male	497	492	500
Female	446	443	453
Race			
African-American	354	332	351
White	493	442	447

Source: U.S. Dept. of Education 1988, table nos. 88 and 89, p. 108.

As mentioned earlier, between 1977 and 1986, the *gap* in participation rates increased for African-Americans and whites enrolled in college. Specifically, although the number of African-American high school graduates 18 to 24 years increased and the number of white high school graduates 18 to 24 years decreased, the college participation rates increased for whites from 33 percent in 1976 to 34.1 percent in 1986 but decreased for African-Americans from 33.4 percent in 1976 to 28.6 percent in 1986. Participation for African-Americans fell to a low of 26.1 percent in 1985 (Wilson and Carter 1988). Similarly, the persistence rate for African-Americans is extremely low. Defined as the attainment of a bachelor's degree within six years, only 25.6 percent of African-Americans had received a B.A. degree, compared to 48 percent of whites after six years at a four-year public institution (Wilson and Carter 1988).

Continuing along the pipeline, the leakage of minority students from the system at the graduate level is so profound that their retention rate is 50 to 75 percent lower than that of white students (Educational Testing Service 1988). Whereas every other minority group increased graduate enrollment in higher education between 1976 and 1986, the percentage of African-Americans decreased from 5.9 percent of the total graduate enrollment in 1976 to 5 percent in 1986. In professional school enrollment, however, African-American participation rates increased slightly, from 4.6 percent in 1976 to 5.2 percent in 1986 (Wilson and Carter 1988). Furthermore, in terms of attaining a degree, the number of African-American students earning M.A.s dropped 32 percent between 1976 and 1985, and the number receiving Ph.D.s dropped 5 percent. Hence, African-American students received a mere 4 percent of *all* doctoral degrees (Educational Testing Service 1988)—tremendous odds!

Explanations of risk and attrition

These data on the achievement gap must be viewed heuristically. Despite recent advances in testing and measurement, it is still impossible to assess how much of the variance in *measured* academic achievement is a consequence of culturally biased tools of measurement (Johnson 1988). The data are sufficient, however, to warrant the conclusion that educational institutions help to create unequal educational opportunity for all students.

Alternative explanations of the academic underpreparedness of minorities and other groups exist. Over recent years, arguments of innate inferiority have been supplanted by "value arguments." That is, some analysts now claim that minorities, in particular African-Americans, do not value education. Research, however, does not support such arguments.

Values regarding aspirations

Some researchers have found that African-American children have high occupational and educational aspirations and that they value academic achievement more highly than white or Mexican-American children (Banks, McQuater, and Hubbard 1978). Further, African-American children report not only a greater desire than whites for a college education but also more encouragement from their parents to pursue a college degree. At the same time, however, African-Americans consistently expressed expectations for success that contrasted with their apparent values and aspirations. In other words, discrepancies occurred between what they desired and what they expected to attain with regard to academic achievement (Banks, McQuater, and Hubbard 1978).

. . . African-American children report not only a greater desire than whites for a college education but also more encouragemnt from their parents . . .

These findings led to the conclusion that the aspirations and value orientations of African-Americans toward academic tasks and traditional achievement-related goals do not account for their relative failure in those domains. It appears that for African-Americans, desires and liking alone may be insufficient to ensure effective orientation toward achievement and success. Thus, what may interfere is the effect of social influence (Banks, McQuater, and Hubbard 1978).

Perceptions of the value of academic achievement

The original value of education as "knowledge" or a tool of learning has been diluted. Nearly 70 percent of today's college students cite economic and financial factors as key motivations for the attainment of their degree. Those who have acquired skills that are in greatest demand are the ones who flourish and succeed. And those belonging to preferred racial groups who are networked into the existing marketplace will be hired faster and earn more.

Minority and disadvantaged students know that these patterns exist from firsthand or secondhand experience. Often their parents, relatives, neighbors, or acquaintances may have experienced these patterns. What is even more discouraging is that some see that their highly qualified parents and role models are sometimes unable to find employment comparable to their skills and qualifications. Indeed, many are unemployed and underemployed (U.S. Dept. of Education 1989). In general, the net present value of the degree is less for a minority than for a white male with a similar degree. Furthermore, the gap widens as the level of education increases. Thus, many very academically capable students may not develop positive attitudes toward school subjects. And as might be expected, a significant positive correlation exists between perceived usefulness of a subject and academic achievement (Johnson and Prom 1984; Jones 1987).

Conclusions and Implications

Educational indicators show that American education is at a crossroads. Schools have succeeded in reversing the negative performance of the 1970s, and basic skills have increased. Yet deficits in higher-order skills remain (Applebee, Langer, and Mullis 1989). Systematic changes are needed across subjects to help students go beyond basic skills to more critical and analytical thinking skills—those skills needed to enter the work force in the next decade and, particularly, the next century.

Although the analysis of the situation is dismal, interventions are possible. Some researchers have found that carefully structured programs designed to enhance productive thinking, self-perceived ability, and self-concept can enhance academic achievement (Johnson and Prom 1984; Resnick 1986).

The central aim is to help students think of themselves as problem solvers and to resist immobilization by the fear of failing (Covington 1985; Whimbey and Lochhead 1984). The program of productive thinking constitutes a model for formal instruction in metacognitive strategies similar to those found in research on information processing or problem solving (Polson and Jeffries 1985).

Enrichment programs geared toward problem solving have been used to improve general intelligence through special training with high school and college students. The programs provide practice and feedback on tasks involving spatial reasoning and on certain kinds of logic tasks that usually appear on intelligence and aptitude tests (Resnick 1986; Whimbey and Lochhead 1984).

Practicing thinking skills in a healthy, interactive educational setting appears to provide students opportunities for trying out new approaches and for social support in valuing efforts, even when they are only partially successful. In this way, students come to think of themselves as capable of analytical thinking, thereby developing a stronger self-perception of their own ability to engage in higher-order thinking (Resnick 1986). Such dispositions require long-term cultivation through skilled instruction in the structure of knowledge required by subjects like mathematics, opportunities for observation and practice, encouragement of students' questioning, and numerous opportunities for success and reinforcement. It is the task of educational administrators and faculty to provide these needed goods to high-risk populations.

NONACADEMIC FACTORS ASSOCIATED
WITH RISK AND ATTRITION

Theory and practice regarding risk and attrition have focused primarily on academic factors. Such a tendency is understandable, given the inherent fallibility of techniques for drawing inferences regarding causality. The academic underpreparedness of many high-risk students is immediately apparent, and sophisticated statistical models are unnecessary to document their academic shortcomings. It has been theorized, however, that nonacademic factors may play a key role in explaining attrition (Pantages and Creedon 1978; Spady 1970; Tinto 1975). Empirical research has also documented the critical role of nonacademic variables. One research team found that academic variables explain less than 50 percent of the difference in behavior between persisters and nonpersisters (Johnson and Richardson 1986). Accordingly, it is critical to examine nonacademic causes and correlates of attrition and risk.

The area of the nonacademic, however, is quite broad. And while existing literature enumerates a number of nonacademic variables associated with risk, no holistic model exists that interrelates risk and attrition with the mechanisms by which social stratification is sustained. Thus, while academic underpreparedness is a major cause of attrition, it is itself a consequence of the interaction of personal, institutional, and systemic factors. The question then is, "How do these categories of factors interact?" The answer is linked to the relationship between risk and social stratification.

The United States is not, of course, a classless society. Those demographic/socioeconomic groups that produce high-risk students do in general experience fewer chances in life. Even education, which has historically played a major role as an instrument of social mobility, is not equally accessible. Social background rather than academic ability is the primary determinant of a student's attendance at an elite college (Karabel and Astin 1975). Other studies of social stratification document that systemic factors continue to shape and contour chances in life (Colasanto and Williams 1987; Watson 1987).

While systemic forces are often "accused" of compliance with the high-risk status of some demographic/socioeconomic groups, references to the process by which systemic forces operate have been quite vague. Some analysts (Collier and Smith 1982; Jones and Watson 1988; Watson and Smith 1987) have argued that the processes that produce attrition and risk

(and other negative by-products of social stratification) function through three major mechanisms:

1. Inherent societal norms that assign people to different strata based on criteria the larger society agrees to.
2. A system of sanctions that urges individuals to choose behaviors consistent with their existing status so that efforts toward mobility generate extraordinary personal stress.
3. A sociocultural ontology buttressed by mythology and folklore that reinforces individual and group perceptions of the superiority of the dominant group.

This section examines nonacademic factors associated with attrition within this framework.

Teachers' Negative Attitudes: The Embodiment of a Race-/Class-/Gender-based Ontology

Theories regarding administrators and teachers are developed within a framework of an ontological system. An ontology refers to a theory of existence or the nature of being. Because the ontology of our society is based on race, gender, and class, teachers and administrators may be socialized and acculturated into a particular belief system with regard to minorities, females, and the disadvantaged. Thus, educational institutions may become an umbrella system or organization from which discrimination and differential treatment are meted out. Subtle forms of discrimination may serve to undermine students' self-esteem, thereby assisting the process of attrition. The ontology of teachers and administrators may create an aversion to high-risk, low-income, and minority students. It is this aversion that can manifest itself in negative attitudes and behaviors toward these students.

A number of studies have documented the operation of this race-based ontology in the classroom. According to one researcher, the process that leads to disproportionate rates of attrition among particular demographic and socioeconomic groups actively begins at age seven (Steere 1984). Further, teachers in combination with movies, literature, and the larger society separate children into "good" and "bad" students. For the most part, entry into each polarized category is based on race/ethnicity and socioeconomic class. But the projection of negative qualities to students by key educational personnel also occurs outside the classroom. Administrative support staff, building engineers, and others can also engage in such behaviors.

Inability to relate to ethnically or culturally different students

Teachers' (and others') negative attitudes are manifested in several forms. In its most extreme form, the race-/gender-/class-based ontology may shape attitudes in such a way that the teacher, administrator, and/or adviser is unable to relate to an ethnically or racially different student. The inability to relate can be expressed by simple prejudgment and subsequent avoidance, or it can assume a more severe form. Some people within the institutional environment may suffer from xenophobia—a fear of and aversion to all who are seen as different and strange (Pettigrew et al. 1982). Xenophobic teachers and administrators may need to avoid all contact with culturally different students. Thus, such students may fail to receive proper academic and personal assistance.

Although high-risk students participate in and share the culture of the wider American society, cultural differences prevail (Akbar 1976; Hale 1982). For example, the special self-expression, oral and aural means of communication, and time-as-social-and-subjective dimension as value orientations distinctive in African-Americans (Boykin 1985) often manifest themselves in their classroom behavior. Further, language barriers, different religious beliefs, and other cultural differences may affect the learning experiences of minority and high-risk students.

Teachers as well as students may have negative or hostile responses to these ethnocultural differences within the student body. Ethnocultural differences tend to be judged harshly against a standard based on the dominant group's culture.

Ethnocentrism, a Eurocentric world view, and a race-/class-/gender-based ontology

Ethnocentrism often characterizes the behavior of service deliverers in institutions of higher education. Ethnocentrism—the belief in the superiority of one's own culture—is, however, differentially applied, and its intensity is a direct function of the apparent and implied differences between the minority and majority group (Pettigrew et al. 1982). Thus, ethnocentric behavior toward African-Americans may be even greater than that directed toward Hispanics and other groups. Several propositions introduced some 45 years ago appear to be useful even today as an explanation of ethnocentric behavior:

1. The stronger the cultural differences between various racial and ethnic groups, the greater the subordination of the minority group.
2. The greater the physical differences between racial and ethnic groups, the greater the subordination of the subordinate race.
3. Significantly divergent cultural and biological traits lead to an intense period of subordination, with assimilation occurring exceptionally slowly (Warner and Strole 1945).

The order of assimilation into American society would then occur along the following lines:

1. Light Caucasoids
2. Dark Caucasoids
3. Mongoloid and Caucasoid mixtures with Caucasoid appearance
4. Negroes and Negroid mixtures (Warner and Strole 1945).

In other words, American society is structured through a socialization process that inculcates different degrees of prejudice and discrimination toward the various ethnic and racial groups (Warner and Strole 1945). Such attitudes then differentially contour the rate at which such groups may develop and exploit their inherent capabilities.

Again, more recent studies of prejudice and discrimination document this trend. Econometric studies have found that *discrimination is a stronger factor with African-Americans than with other ethnic groups.* One study (Gwartney and Long 1978), for example, found that when minorities are "matched" with their white counterparts in terms of education as well as other variables of the labor market, the differential is greatest for African-Americans. Japanese-Americans in the study earned only 11 percent less than their white counterparts and Mexican-Americans only 9 percent less, but African-Americans earned 21 percent less (Gwartney and Long 1978).

Ethnocentrism and the Eurocentric world view also affect the academic content of courses. Today, even textbooks in a number of fields include unflattering and inaccurate information regarding other groups. Some economic textbooks cite the increase in females' and minorities' participation rates in the labor force as a cause of decreased productivity. It is conceivable that the use of ethnocentric and Eurocentric textbooks may indirectly enhance dropout rates.

The concept of a race-/gender-/class-based ontology transcends the concept of discrimination. This ontology is characterized by a set of behaviors, beliefs, and axioms regarding the "place" of various groups in society. Thus, a teacher may unconsciously view a poor minority child who wishes to become a mathematician as an inversion of the natural order of things. Simultaneously, the teacher may see truancy among poor minority children as part of the natural order. This intellectual structure may be so subtle and embedded that even the most culturally sensitive teacher or administrator is unaware of its operation.

The Psychodynamics of Systemic Forces: The Impact of Low Self-esteem and the Self-fulfilling Prophecy

In addition to systemic factors explaining risk and attrition, students' individual factors must also be considered. Poor study habits and academic underpreparedness represent a failure by the student to acquire needed skills. Yet teachers' negative attitudes, an ethnocentric classroom environment, and a Eurocentric society do place undue burden upon students, creating a failure of their coping mechanisms. Thus, they fail to complete their degrees. Why do some students persist in similar circumstances? This question raises the issue of intermediating variables. What are the mechanisms that transmit environmental influences into the behavior guidance system of the individual?

While a number of alternative explanations can be used, self-esteem and self-concept are often cited as intermediating variables between systemic and behavioral factors (Jones and Watson 1988). Environmental forces can lead to low aspirations and low self-esteem. Thus, teachers' and administrators' negative attitudes can also lead to low self-esteem, which in turn may cause students to "cooperate" with systemic forces.

Low self-esteem

Teachers, administrators, and counselors directly affect students' self-esteem, which in turn affects their performance. Several researchers have documented these relationships. While high-risk students who do succeed perceive themselves as self-confident as well as self-motivated (Geary 1988), teachers' attitudes have been found to have a much stronger effect on academic achievement than either the student's or the teacher's perceptions of the student's ability (Holliday 1985), particularly with African-American students.

Other studies have linked the importance of teachers' affective behaviors with students' self-concept. One study explored the relationship between teachers' affective cues and the self-perception of sixth graders by race and socioeconomic status (Graham 1984). In that study, middle-class African-American children had the most positive self-concept in the pretest, but all racial and socioeconomic groups in the sample changed their self-perceptions in response to teachers' affective cues.

Teachers, however, are not the sole determinants of their students' self-esteem. Systemic forces combined with psychogenic traits shape self-esteem. One study of self-concept and economic disadvantage, for example, found that disadvantaged African-American students had the lowest self-concept of all groups in the sample (Bledsoe and Dixon 1980). Another study found that white children have higher ideal self-images and greater image disparity than African-Americans (Phillips and Zigler 1980). Higher ideal selves lead to higher aspirations. For example, white males with high self-concepts have higher educational goals (Zuckerman 1980). On the other hand, even some gifted African-American children have lower self-images than their counterparts of other races (Brown, Fulkerson, et al. 1983; Tidwell 1980).

Problems related to self-esteem as an intermediating variable are not insurmountable. Small groups, for example, can be used as a method of psychosocial intervention (Brown 1984), but other strategies have also been used.

Self-concept, once damaged, however, may be difficult to repair. One intervention program found that even as the writing skills of African-American students improved to the level of white students, African-American students maintained expectations of weak performance (McCarthy and Meir 1983).

The negative impact of an ethnocentric environment on self-esteem tends to cross racial and ethnic boundaries. White students have reported a similar loss of self-esteem when placed within the context of an Afrocentric world, experiencing frustration, ineffective coping, and subsequent loss of esteem, for example, as the single white member of an African-American high school basketball team (Bromberg 1984).

Acceptance of the self-fulfilling prophecy

The overcrowded, poverty-ridden conditions in which many high-risk children grow and develop engender low aspirations and low expectations of life in general. Many of the children and adults are preoccupied with satisfying their primary needs for food and shelter. Their physical environment may be in disarray, and their social environment may include crime and violence. Thus, their coping mechanisms are focused on survival, and the low expectations of self as well as others become self-fulfilling prophecies. Attrition is the fulfillment of risk and the fulfillment of the prophecy.

At the high school level, attrition exceeds the rates in institutions of higher education. Depending on the source of information and the method of estimation, the high school dropout rate varies from 15 percent to 27 percent (U.S. Dept. of Education 1988). For African-Americans, the dropout rate has reached epidemic proportions nationally. In some urban areas, dropout rates have been as high as 47 percent for Hispanics and 61 percent for African-Americans (Hammack 1986).

Cooperating with "Oppression": Social Dynamics Related to Attrition

The antisocial behaviors exhibited by many youth may be a reflection of these broader social issues. The factors described above interact to limit opportunities for social mobility and to cause particular demographic or social economic groups to become at risk. Additionally, such students come from families with multiple stressors. Thus, pregnancy, secondary school dropouts, and juvenile delinquency represent this process.

Teenage pregnancy

While a correlation exists between pregnancy and attrition in higher education, its magnitude is superseded by the relationship between attrition and pregnancy at the secondary level. Thus, educators and policy analysts have directed considerable attention toward pregnancy as a major cause of attrition among high school girls. The prevalence of sexual activity, pregnancy, and child bearing among teenagers in the

United States is well documented. In 1987, 472,623 babies were born to teenagers, and approximately two-thirds of those births were out of wedlock (Moore 1989). Another 40 percent of pregnant teenagers terminated the pregnancy through abortion. It is projected that by 2000, nearly 20 percent of all teenage girls will have given birth to at least one child (Moore 1989).

Teenage pregnancy not only directly increases the probability of attrition but also perpetuates risk and attrition in another way. That is, teenagers are likely to give birth to low-birth-weight or premature babies, whose chances of survival beyond the first year are very slim. Further, many of those infants who do survive may experience problems with school learning and be classified as mentally retarded or learning disabled.

Dropouts and "pushouts"
Many students never experience the opportunity to be a college statistic, for they do not complete high school. Some students, however, are pushouts rather than dropouts. The quality and success of a school system can often be judged by the numbers or percentages of its students who attend school and graduate. It has been well documented (particularly during the "school reform" era) that when schools fail to stimulate the mental processes of their students, truancy and attrition may occur.

Truancy (unexcused absence from school) has hitherto been regarded as a misdemeanor engaged in by a relatively small percentage of the school population. More recently, however, truancy has become a major social problem that leads to dropping out of school. The impersonal atmosphere created by large classes, multiple course offerings, and the use of many teachers at the secondary level may be factors that encourage truancy (Sentelle 1980). Often, too, these conditions mean that those students who are not doing well in their classes are at greater risk of failure.

Some reasons for students' dropping out have been elevated above others. Repeating a grade, a school atmosphere stressing silence, order, control, and competition, and instructional styles incompatible with the learning styles of at-risk students are factors that explain the greatest amount of variance (Tuck 1988). A recent study of an urban public school system reported that 55 percent of the dropouts left school before they reached 10th grade and 80 percent left before 11th grade. Furthermore, 5 percent of dropouts had been retained in grades more than once, approximately 75 percent lived in single-parent homes, over 50 percent reported that they quit school because they kept failing, and one-third blamed the school climate (Tuck 1988).

These findings support those of previous studies. Teenage pregnancy, crime, poverty, and other variables are directly related to attrition among high school students. Chief among the list of variables cited for attrition are the student's socioeconomic status and educational experiences in school. The high school dropout, like his or her collegiate counterpart, tends to be from a family of low socioeconomic status where the parents are in low-paying jobs and are relatively uneducated. The attrition rate for students with fathers in lower-level occupations was 115 percent greater than the rate for students whose fathers were in high-level occupations (U.S. Dept. of Education 1981).

Another social correlate of high school dropouts is a one-parent household and a large family. If the one parent is female, the dropout rate is 66 percent higher—if the parent is male, 78 percent higher—than when both parents are present. When both parents are absent, the dropout rate is two and one-half times greater than the rate when both parents live at home. Dropout rates for students from families with seven or more siblings are significantly higher than for students from smaller families, although a notable exception is for students who are only children in the family, where the dropout rate is higher than for students with one to three siblings (U.S. Dept. of Education 1981).

High school nonpersisters' parents often themselves have a low level of education, and many have been dropouts. Children whose parents dropped out of school are three to five times more at risk of dropping out than are students from advanced backgrounds. Students whose fathers are only high school graduates are about 100 percent more likely to drop out than students whose fathers have four or more years of higher education. Those children whose fathers did not finish high school are nearly 250 percent more likely to drop out. The mother's education is also negatively related to dropout rates (U.S. Dept. of Education 1981).

Other correlates of high school attrition may also hold for nonpersisters in higher education. The profile of dropouts'

. . . if they are not provided with meaningful and positive learning experiences, many [students] will develop and exhibit negative behaviors.

educational experiences is that the dropout typically performs poor academically, has discipline problems, and is delinquent. Like college, the student's academic performance and progress can be used to identify students at risk of dropping out (U.S. Dept. of Education 1981). Attrition rates are higher for students with the lowest test scores. Students who score in the lowest ability quartile are eight times more likely to drop out than students with scores in the ability quartile. In addition, students who have had disciplinary problems in school, have been suspended or placed on probation, or have been "in trouble" with the law are about three times more likely to drop out than students who have not had such problems (Sentelle 1980; Tuck 1988; U.S. Dept. of Education 1987).

Some other characteristics of the dropout are related to marriage, child bearing, and employment while in school: Dropout rates are higher for students who are married, have children, or both, and for students who work while in school.

Juvenile delinquency

If students' minds are not stimulated during their time at school and if they are not provided with meaningful and positive learning experiences, many will develop and exhibit negative behaviors. When students drop out of school, all too often they have few prospects of meaningful and gainful employment. Thus, left with large amounts of idle time, many choose crime and delinquency to survive. A primary contemporary form of delinquency involves drugs, which are responsible for a major portion of the crime in urban neighborhoods. Even the type of crimes committed has become more serious and violent today than in years past. Teenage crime has shifted from petty theft and truancy to assault, murder, and extortion. For example, approximately 52.2 percent of all arrests involving African-American teenagers under age 18 were for violent crimes, and 26.6 percent involved drug abuse (U.S. Dept. of Justice 1987).

While substantial research exists on crime and delinquency for high school nonpersisters, little research has been conducted regarding crime and delinquency as a correlate of attrition in higher education. Additional research is needed in this area.

Conclusions and Implications

It is clear that the academic experiences of high-risk students cannot be divorced from the influences of the larger society.

Nonacademic factors also play a significant role in creating the conditions for risk and attrition. Race and class limit and structure chances in general, ultimately directly or indirectly affecting the ability of many minorities to obtain quality education and in turn creating a vicious cycle of underdevelopment for high-risk students. Without education, high-risk students have little hope of escaping their depressed social conditions.

Socioeconomic status affects the multiple social correlates of attrition and risk (e.g., family structure, self-esteem, teenage pregnancy). In addition, many such students find postsecondary education to be a less than viable option because of the rising cost of education and the limited availability of grants. And the undereducation of high-risk students obliterates their futures as productive participants in the wider society.

The elimination of the status of high risk requires both academic and nonacademic solutions. Government, private industry, and a variety of community organizations must make a concerted effort to equalize societal opportunities overall. Only in this way can the phenomenon of high risk be curbed.

STRATEGIES FOR ACHIEVING SUCCESS AMONG HIGH-RISK STUDENTS BY THE 21st CENTURY

Students in institutions of higher education do encounter risk, and that risk assumes several forms. It may involve a higher probability of a low grade point average, a relatively greater probability of choosing a field that is incongruent with the skills and competencies needed by the labor market of the 21st century, and/or a greater chance of not completing the college degree. Thus, the potential for risk and attrition exists for all college enrollees. For some populations, however, the probabilities of risk and attrition are extraordinarily high.

A number of causal variables interact to increase attrition and risk among particular demographic and socioeconomic populations. These variables, as previously discussed, may include academic factors (e.g., low GPA and academic underpreparedness) but may extend far beyond the scope of the academic. Indeed, each high-risk student represents the outcome of his or her individual characteristics in combination with the shaping and contouring that occur as a consequence of a socially stratified society.

Attrition and risk, however, are both directly and indirectly costly. Moreover, the population of historically disadvantaged groups is increasing in society. Simultaneously, the need for a larger and better-trained work force is increasing. Thus, it becomes critical to design strategies for intervention to ameliorate risk and attrition.

While colleges and universities have been disproportionately responsible for the development of such strategies, reducing attrition and risk requires that each actor within the society assume a share of the responsibility. Thus, high-risk students themselves must be challenged to develop the academic and nonacademic skills and competencies associated with collegiate "success." Administrators, teachers, advisers and counselors, and other students, however, are also required to engage in behaviors to reduce the probability of risk among high-risk groups. Institutions of higher education must not only create programs but also financially and morally commit themselves to address the needs of high-risk students. Last, businesses, community action groups, and other organizations have roles in addressing this critical problem.

Indeed, each of these agents has been involved in the development and implementation of strategies to reduce risk. Of greater importance, many of the strategies in use do work. For example, a meta-analysis of the results of 60 collegiate

programs designed to assist high-risk students found that, for the most part, strategies to reduce attrition increase persistence and improve GPA (Kulik, Kulik, and Shwalb 1983). The improvement in attrition was smaller than expected, however. A similar study also found that strategies to reduce attrition reduced it even though the reduction was small (Schmedinghoff 1979).

Nevertheless, efforts continue. A number of colleges and universities have integrated the reduction of risk into their strategic management plans. Some institutions, Florida Community College at Jacksonville, for example, have implemented programs to manage enrollment (Spence 1988). Such programs seek to apply the systematic tools of management science to the problems of risk and attrition. In some cases, a program to manage enrollment involves the creation of a specific organizational unit for the planning, execution, coordination, and control of all recruiting and retention. At other times, existing units perform these activities. An alternative approach used by the Virginia community college system emphasizes marketing as well as management through a marketing and retention recognition program (Puyear 1987a, b).

Such programs explore the needs and wants of their target population and seek to design an appropriate "marketing mix" for the target market. The development of an appropriate marketing mix involves the reevaluation of the institution's products and product offerings and greater attention to promotion. Such an approach increases persistence by enhancing consistency between the institution (the supplier) and the student (the client). Common to each of these approaches, however, is a high level of institutional commitment to the resolution of the problems that produce risk and attrition.

While all efforts to enhance the success rates of high-risk students do not occur under the auspices of a comprehensive institutional mandate, a vast number of colleges and universities across the country do engage and/or have engaged in strategies to reduce risk.

Identifying Special Needs for Retention among High-risk Students

Inevitably, prescription must be preceded by analysis. Thus, before programs and initiatives to reduce risk are designed, those students who are subject to risk must be identified. Equally important, colleges and universities must not only know which of their students are subject to risk but must also assess the special retention needs of each segment of their high-risk population. Again, such involvement requires a high level of commitment by these institutions (Van Allen 1988).

Institutional commitment
Developing strategies to reduce risk and increase the likelihood of retention and attaining a degree requires commitment by the institution. Institutional commitment can be evaluated using several criteria: admissions and recruitment, financial aid, counseling, support services and placement, curriculum, and environment (Crosson 1987). A number of different administrative models have emerged to catalyze institutional support for retention.

An evaluation of successful efforts to improve the achievement of degrees by minority students at 10 predominantly white four-year institutions revealed that the majority of those institutions had six characteristics in common:

1. They had strong programs to help students with problems in academic preparation.
2. They emphasized precollege programs and had developed relations with elementary and secondary schools.
3. They emphasized multicultural environments.
4. They successfully resolved the organizational dilemma of separatist versus support programs for minority students.
5. They developed proactive approaches to financial aid.
6. They provided opportunities for on-campus housing (Crosson 1987).

For public institutions, the creation of strategies to reduce risk and attrition has sometimes been driven by the state. The state of California, for example, has incorporated expanded educational opportunity for Hispanics into its basic objectives and goals (Fields 1987). Thus, the state ensures that colleges and universities are provided at least minimal resources for increasing equal educational opportunities among this growing population. A number of other public institutions with retention programs also have the moral and financial backing of their sources of funding.

Still other institutions are so highly committed to retention that they have formed consortia. Such consortia might convene at regular intervals to compare, contrast, and brainstorm strategies to reduce attrition. Community colleges in Oregon and Washington, for example, organize an annual conference in which they focus on strategies to reduce risk. A valuable part of this collaboration is the production and distribution of a directory that contains the results of evaluating existing strategies (Greene et al. 1987).

Thus, in some instances, strategies to reduce attrition and risk become driven by the institution. Managing enrollment, as mentioned, is an approach that incorporates goals and activities for retention into the very essence of institutional mission. California State University at Los Angeles, for example, places its retention activities within the context of enrollment management (Dolence et al. 1988).

Some colleges and universities may have internally driven activities to reduce risk without a formalized commitment to retention. It appears, however, that high levels of institutional commitment tend to lead to the development of comprehensive strategies addressing a broad range of the causes and correlates of attrition. A synthesis of the research on multiple causes of students' attrition theorizes that a student's departure from college should serve as a barometer of the institution's social and intellectual health as well as the student's experiences at the institution (Tinto 1987). Thus, the level of faculty-student interaction and a student's integration into the school are central factors in attrition.

Mount St. Mary's College in Los Angeles has a special campus for high-risk students. The Doheny Campus, which actually segregates high-risk students, consists of a comprehensive structure for addressing the academic and nonacademic needs of this population before reintegrating them into the main collegiate program (Kelly 1988). The program incorporates every necessary element for reducing risk: outreach, the development of skills, academic reinforcement, a monitoring system, tutorials, advising and counseling, and special attention to multicultural differences among students.

While other colleges and universities have not adopted separate campuses (which may have the unforeseen consequence of stigmatizing students), a number of other institutions have comprehensive retention programs. Some of the special services offered include remedial classes, tutoring by peers, student leadership, and academic counseling, among others. When done effectively, these programs work synergistically to increase academic and nonacademic skills as well as the student's sense of belonging.

Some colleges have used marketing segmentation in their development of a comprehensive program for reducing risk. Marketing segmentation is based on the notion that different demographic groups may have different needs. Thus, while some institutions may have a broad program to retain minorities (Clewell 1987), they may structure specialized programs for specific minority groups. California State University at Fresno, the University of North Carolina at Greensboro, Boston College, and Purdue University each offer comprehensive programs for the retention of high-risk African-American and Hispanic students (Collison 1987).

In contrast, Indiana University in Bloomington has a special program for the retention of talented African-American students on its campus (Vaz 1987). Such students neither are underprepared nor have low SAT scores. Rather, the risks associated with their tenure on a white campus may be increased because of financial and/or environmental factors. Comprehensive programs have also been designed to accommodate the needs of adult students. Wayne Community College in Michigan has implemented such a program, for example (Goldman 1981).

Finally, partnerships between schools and colleges have also been used as institutional frameworks for the design and creation of retention programs. These partnerships are critical, because such a framework provides the opportunity for reducing risk before the student actually enters the higher educational pipeline. Summaries of almost 85 school-college partnership programs directed toward reducing educational risk for gifted and talented as well as for academically underprepared students point out that a high level of organizational commitment makes such comprehensive programs possible (Wilbur 1988). Organizational commitment, however, must be combined with intensive outreach so that the needs of high-risk students can be identified, assessed, and serviced.

Intensive outreach
Outreach to retain high-risk populations must be preceded by efforts to recruit these groups of students into institutions of higher education. A number of recommendations for the recruitment of minorities by colleges of education (Krajewski and Simmons 1988) are also applicable to the recruitment

of high-risk students into other fields that may offer greater opportunities by 2000. Community-based organizations can also be significant agents for the recruitment of high-risk students (Dunn 1987).

The recruitment of high-risk students is intimately linked with procedures and criteria for admissions. Educators are quite familiar with the debate regarding the validity of SAT and ACT scores for minorities, females, and the disadvantaged. It is also generally accepted that, for these groups, grades are a more accurate predictor of academic performance than aptitude test scores. Nevertheless, institutions of higher education are confronted with the task of constructing admissions standards that do not automatically bypass the applications of students who are high risk.

Some institutions have resorted to the use of an expert systems model in making decisions about admissions (Diffenbac 1987). This model combines quantitative indices of academic success with qualitative indices. More specifically, an expert systems model involves a computer simulation program that analyzes previous decisions about admissions and then makes new decisions based on the logic and/or illogic of past decisions. While the model has not been tested at the undergraduate level, its predictive powers have been high at the graduate level.

A stated major strength of the expert systems model is its ability to demand consistency in decisions about admissions. It could, however, also be a shortcoming of the model, because profiles of high-risk students are such that qualitative, subjective decision making must sometimes take precedence over logic. An expert systems approach eliminates the possibility of such a choice.

Once students have been admitted, outreach can be directed toward identifying those students whose profiles indicate above-average risk. This process can actually begin at registration. Some colleges use registration as a tool of outreach for identifying and beginning a relationship with high-risk students (Martin 1987). A Pennsylvania community college reportedly conducts enrollment, placement testing, and academic advising within a single day. (In some cases, students and families are involved in the process.) Thus, within a day of registration, sufficient data are available for the identification of at-risk students (Martin 1987).

Outreach designed to identify high-risk students is perhaps easier to design than outreach for the assessment of needs. Nevertheless, some successful models do exist. Testing instruments like the Scholastic Aptitude Test, the Effective Study Test, the Myers-Briggs Type Indicator, and other academic and nonacademic testing tools have been used to assess the needs of high-risk students (Nisbet 1982). Again, however, care must be taken to choose the most valid assessment instruments.

The University of Maryland Counseling Center has devised a distinctive approach for assessing the needs of poorly performing students. Specifically, the center in 1984 used group counseling to assess the needs of students with a GPA below 2.0. Additionally, the experiment was designed to determine whether attrition rates would differ for students who were contacted by the center through the outreach program and those who decided independently to participate in the diagnostic and prescriptive interviews. As might be expected, students who voluntarily participated in the sessions showed greater improvement in their GPAs than those students recruited through outreach (Boyd 1988). (The results, however, could be the result of selection bias in the sample.)

Far too little attention has been directed toward another critical area. More research is needed on the information-processing styles of ethnic minorities. As mentioned earlier, failure to provide students with stimulating and challenging learning experiences can lead to attrition and risk. The College of Education at Southern Illinois University–Carbondale, for example, based one of its programs to deal with attrition on an assessment of learning styles. Advisers used various diagnostic tests and individual counseling to assist each student in the program in identifying his or her cognitive learning style. In that way, students were able to participate more proactively in increasing their GPAs. The program resulted in a positive evaluation (Jenkins et al. 1981).

Outreach could, however, be required to monitor students' progress *before* they experience poor academic performance. For instance, a number of variables could be used as signals of a potential problem: a history of academic trouble, large numbers of absences, problems in basic composition, deficient note-taking skills, and so on. Teachers and advisers may be given the responsibility of referring students experiencing such problems to a remedial program.

. . . profiles of high-risk students are such that qualitative, subjective decision making must sometimes take precedence over logic.

Finally, outreach should include follow-up of those students who did not persist. A number of colleges and universities already have such programs in place (Smurthwaite 1977). Most colleges with follow-up programs contact both persisters and nonpersisters to compare and contrast the two groups.

Quite innovative is a program at William Rainey Harper College, which follows up on students who withdrew from and/or failed an introductory criminal justice course that was the prerequisite for a number of other courses (Evans and Lucas 1988). Strategies of this type are particularly appropriate for retention in mathematics and science courses.

Building and enhancing self-esteem

One particular need for high-risk students may involve the enhancement of low self-esteem. As mentioned earlier, high-risk students could internalize their perceived failures and consequently develop low self-esteem. A self-perpetuating cycle can then emerge, because low self-esteem is highly correlated with anxiety, passivity, and an array of other nonadaptive behaviors.

A number of colleges and universities appear to recognize that achievement and the enhancement of self-esteem are mutually dependent. Thus, some programs have been designed to enhance self-esteem as a means of improving performance. A program at West Virginia University integrated the self-concept of students into advising and counseling. The goal of this strategy was to promote self-management skills in high-risk students (Pawlicki and Connell 1981). The University of Tennessee at Knoxville used a comprehensive approach that included improved self-esteem as one of its objectives (Sidel and McCullough 1980). Similarly, the special services program of the University of Minnesota's General College found that enhanced self-esteem was a by-product of the comprehensive program to reduce attrition (Reed 1982). Students' involvement in campus activities is empowering and could therefore raise self-esteem and increase persistence (Webb 1987).

Academic Support Services

Once the broad-based needs of high-risk students have been identified, it is possible to create strategies to address them. High-risk students need considerable academic enhancement, and a number of programs have been established over the years to upgrade the academic achievement of high-risk students. Programs have also been established to build the more general skills that help to create academic excellence—study habits, taking notes, and so forth.

Developing and building skills

Even before the emergence of high-risk students on college campuses, administrators recognized that many students require assistance to enhance the transition from high school to college. Thus, traditional college orientation courses emerged. Although such courses probably did reduce risk, earlier orientation courses did not include a means of evaluation and the results could not be documented. Nevertheless, orientation courses have continued to be used to familiarize students with college life and thereby reduce risk (Banich 1988). Evaluation of the impact of a one-credit orientation course at Miami-Dade Community College, for example, indicates positive effects on retention for those enrolled in the orientation course (Belcher 1987).

During the early seventies, orientation courses were supplemented by special courses targeted toward building basic skills in reading, writing, and mathematics. Such courses, called "compensatory" and/or "remedial," sought primarily to build reading and writing skills (Hechinger 1979; Lifschutz 1982; Losak et al. 1982; Warming 1980). Courses of this type continued to be prevalent through the 1970s and into the 1980s.

Eventually, remediation expanded beyond the basics to include critical thinking, efficient study skills, and specific programs to emphasize academic management (Warming 1980). For example, a program at Grambling State University in Louisiana attempted to reduce risk by teaching high-risk students how to register and withdraw from courses (Riles 1980). Elsewhere, specific programs were created for high-risk students enrolled in courses developed especially for them (Dale 1981).

Courses offered to teach skills development are quite sophisticated now. Further, freshman orientation, once a one-credit course, is now a three-credit course at some schools (Greene 1987). And the content has been expanded. On some campuses, skills in human relations as well as study skills are included in the orientation course (Greene 1987). The effectiveness of these programs is now measured through carefully developed evaluation research.

Academic reinforcement

While the skills needed for persistence and success extend beyond the academic, basic academic competencies must be reinforced. Thus, several administrative issues have emerged regarding academic remediation programs. More specifically, advisers and counselors have sought to ascertain how to structure such programs to provide sufficient academic reinforcement. A major issue is whether remediation should be made mandatory. A number of institutions have resolved this issue by making participation in an academic program to develop skills mandatory for high-risk populations. A recent study of remedial programs in the Michigan community college system found that compulsory programs are positively correlated with persistence over the long term. Voluntary participants, however, excelled in academic achievement in the short term (Lum and Alfred 1987).

Some colleges have sought to reinforce academic skills by combining mandatory participation in remedial programs with mandatory restrictions on enrollment in courses. Again, evaluations indicate that persistence is increased and risk reduced by the requirement for mandatory participation (Walleri 1987). Mandatory participation can, however, create problems. First, it can reduce students' motivation to complete the degree, for the rate of progression may be slower. Second, mandatory participation can create scheduling problems for administrators. And third, the extra credits required may increase the direct costs of the degree (Mitchell 1987). Thus, the benefits of mandatory remediation must be measured against the potential cost.

Another technique that has been used to reinforce the academic skills of both traditional and high-risk students is the integration of various skills into the standard course curriculum. Across-the-curriculum programs are now quite popular. San Diego State University, for example, integrated reading and writing components into all of its general education courses (Denman 1983).

For minority students, academic reinforcement may require special attention to their cultural background. Manhattan Community College has developed a special bilingual program for the reinforcement of academic skills among Hispanic students (Borsi and Rogg 1986). Valencia Community College includes an African-American history course as part of the remediation program for African-Americans (Valencia Community College 1987). Such an approach is based on the belief that academic skills are more easily reinforced when content and context are culturally familiar.

Other strategies have also been used. Some experiments, for example, have indicated that efforts to improve speech communication may reinforce the academic skills of all students (Gwin and Downey 1980). In addition, tutorials and learning labs have been effective tools for students' academic reinforcement (Hirschorn 1988; Vincent 1983).

Social Support

For individual growth and change to occur, individuals and their physical/human/organizational environment must be complementary to a certain degree. Even the most academically superior student may withdraw from an academic environment characterized by isolation. Thus, it is critical that institutions create strategies designed to provide a social support system for high-risk students. This support system should include the major human elements within the environment—administrators, advisers and counselors, family, teachers, and other students.

Administrators

Administrators execute institutional policies; indeed, they have the responsibility to mandate that retention become the highest priority in their institutions. It is therefore imperative that administrators be sensitive to the special needs of high-risk students and be willing to develop and implement strategies to increase these students' retention rates and their levels of academic achievement (see, e.g., Banich 1988; Greene 1987; Lum and Alfred 1987).

Advisers and counselors

The wide range of needs of high-risk students is such that traditional advising and counseling strategies will not always suffice. Thus, it is necessary for counselors and advisers to understand the multidimensional forces that interact to produce risk before they can provide social support to these populations. Advisers and counselors are morally mandated to become knowledgeable regarding the causes and correlates of attrition and risk (Wooldridge 1982), and such knowledge can permit the creation of appropriate social support systems.

Based on an analysis of the needs of high-risk students, some strategists have advocated a very proactive stance for advisers and counselors. Activist-counseling in which counselors initiate the relationship has been found to promote greater persistence than more traditional techniques (Arrington and Romano 1980). More recently, such proactive approaches have been called "intrusive advising" (Lopez et al. 1988).

Family

Brooklyn College has devised a family-centered strategy for social support. The Take Advantage Now/Parent Education Project uses a series of workshops to provide information on the skills and behaviors that correlate with persistence (Walters 1987). Parents are alerted to the relationship between persistence and study habits, financial aid, and related variables. This information then becomes a basis for parents' greater participation as social support in the student's life.

Faculty

Faculty are key links in the range of factors that may elevate risk for some students. Teachers' negative attitudes and inappropriate instructional techniques are two variables that may promote risk, for example. Thus, faculty have the potential to provide critical social support.

Interventions involving faculty can be quite broadly based. For example, faculty can provide support to high-risk students by varying their instructional approaches. Improved strategies could involve broadening techniques so that methods other than lectures are used. In addition, teaching content and style should be matched with objectives for teaching. Moreover, ongoing monitoring of students' progress through diagnostic quizzes and assignments could support retention. Individualized instructional techniques have been found to be particularly effective with high-risk students (Ludwig 1977).

Innovative teaching techniques and a heightened sensitivity to the support needed by high-risk students do not occur automatically. They must be driven by the institution. For example, one school organized a university faculty institute to train teachers in the instructional management of classes containing high-risk students. The institute addressed teachers' attitudes as well as instructional techniques (McPhail 1978). An alternative approach involved the use of team-taught courses in which a learning specialist designs and instructs the course in conjunction with the primary instructor (Harding 1980).

Institutions and faculty must work together to transform faculty members into "trained facilitators" rather than lecturers (Thoren 1987). As such, they could design courses that empower students by involving them as active participants. Among the techniques used is instruction by peers, both individuals and groups. Such interactive teaching techniques would, of course, require relatively small classes.

Another effective means of social support for faculty is individualized and/or institutionally sponsored mentoring. Glendale Community College in Arizona has designed a mentoring program in which participating faculty choose or are assigned a minority student protege. The faculty members act as personal friends and advisers to the students. As expected, some positive results have been recorded (Mendoza and Samuels 1987). Evergreen Valley College in San Jose, California, has a similar program (Maestas-Flores and Chavez 1987).

Students helping students
A truly holistic approach to providing social support to high-risk students must also involve other students. While other students can be indirectly involved in providing support to high-risk students by maintaining compassionate and non-judgmental attitudes, possibilities for a more direct role also exist. Indeed, students can be encouraged to tutor other students (Chapman 1982). In this way, both students' skills are strengthened in the process. Tutoring and peer mentoring programs are valuable at all levels of the educational pipeline (Payne 1987; Smith 1987). Such interaction among administrators, advisers and counselors, parents, teachers, and students can indeed make the college campus a more hospitable environment for high-risk students.

Financial support
Attrition and risk have implications for the funding of colleges and universities. The relationship is a direct one, for the financial formula that determines funding is linked to full-time enrollment (Cross 1983). A certain circular pattern characterizes this relationship, however. If institutions of higher education do not have sufficient funding to provide financial assistance to low-income students, attrition and risk will in-

crease. Because a number of academic and nonacademic factors are associated with risk and attrition, financial assistance alone will not reduce risk.

Schools with large numbers of disadvantaged students enrolled have disproportionately high default rates for repaying loans (*Chronicle* 1989). To a large extent, defaulters are students who dropped out after one academic year. And students who drop out are disproportionately disadvantaged (U.S. Congress 1988). Nevertheless, financial aid must be provided to these populations. Funding for Pell grants and support services is more important than ever as the 21st century approaches. Long-term financial aid promotes persistence (Woodward 1988), for such financial incentives induce students not only to enroll but also to persist and graduate (Fischer 1987).

Financial responsibility for high-risk students is not, however, the exclusive domain of institutions of higher education and their existing sponsors. Because businesses will be direct beneficiaries of reduced risk and increased educational opportunity, it is not surprising that the number of business and educational partnerships is growing. For example, colleges and universities now offer on-site courses for business employees and managers, and businesses now provide financial aid and other support for high-risk students in primary and secondary schools and in colleges and universities (Hixson 1982). Some companies identify high-risk students in secondary schools, investing in their preparation for college and then paying the tuition when the students enroll in college (Bailey 1988). An acceleration of such strategies should be encouraged.

Conclusions and Implications

Based on this evidence, it is clear that high-risk students can succeed. The most successful programs have a holistic, programmatic thrust. First, they demonstrate institutional commitment through the provision of both human and fiscal resources to implement programs that develop academic skills. English and mathematics are primary components of such programs. As students' skills improve, their academic self-concept also improves. Second, these institutions develop a monitoring system that is crucial to students' progress. Such monitoring serves several functions. For example, it provides feedback to students on their progress and facilitates necessary remediation. It also serves as a mechanism of evaluation for program staff; that is, it indicates the effectiveness of the program and identifies areas that need modification and/or change. A third strategy important to the success of high-risk students is the provision of social support. For many of these students, social support provides feelings of security and improves self-confidence and a sense of belonging.

In addition to the various strategies mentioned, advisers and faculty can serve as intellectual mentors. They play key roles in the lives of students and must therefore be sensitive and responsive to the needs of high-risk students. Administrators, the family, and other students are also critical elements. They can offer encouragement, enabling these students to persist in their personal commitment to complete their degrees. In short, the more holistic the program's approach, the greater the likelihood of success for high-risk students.

HIGH-RISK STUDENTS AND HIGHER EDUCATION: Future Trends

Numerous initiatives, policies, and programs currently exist in recognition of the fact that high degrees of risk characterize the collegiate experience of some demographic and socioeconomic groups (Pascarella and Terenzini 1975). Nevertheless, the severity of the problem has not diminished (Kulik, Kulik, and Shwalb 1983). If one aggregates the level of risk that attenuates the educational experience at every level, the conclusion is warranted that levels of risk and attrition were higher in the eighties than in the seventies (Jones 1989a).

It is perhaps this aspect of the problem of risk that is most threatening to future efforts. Past efforts have been relatively great; past successes have been positive but nevertheless disappointing. Thus, college administrators are beginning to ask, "Where do we go from here?" The review of literature on risk and attrition and the alternative perspectives offered in this monograph provide some tentative answers.

Risk and Attrition: A Summary of Findings

Attrition creates social and financial losses for the student, for the institution of higher education, and for the larger society. Attrition, however, is largely the product of risk, and implicit in the notion of risk is the statistical concept of probability. Students with higher probabilities of failing to obtain their academic goals can be described as high-risk and/or at-risk students.

Attrition, however, is a final outcome, and intermediate levels and types of risk are preliminary to attrition. Risk of a low GPA, failure to progress through the curriculum at a "normal" rate, and underperformance in one's major field and the subsequent changing of major are all forms of risk that might or might not lead to attrition. These intermediate forms of risk do, however, adversely affect the student's life and the strategic planning processes of those institutions serving them. Thus, rather than focusing only on retention and attrition, colleges and universities must direct programs and strategies toward risk in its multiple forms.

Programs and strategies cannot, however, be designed without some descriptive knowledge of high-risk populations. And the literature does provide a comprehensive portrait of those enrollees who might embody high-risk characteristics (Astin 1975; Cohen and Brauer 1982; Pruitt 1979).

While "nontraditional" and "high risk" have been used as interchangeable referents (Astin 1975), the terms have different denotations. "Nontraditional" can be used to describe adult enrollees (Cross 1979; Pinkston 1987); thus, all nontraditional students are not high risk. Indeed, some adult enrollees have over recent years outperformed traditional enrollees.

Nevertheless, some adult students do embody characteristics elevating risk (Pinkston 1987): gender (Sheridan 1982; Starks 1987), race and ethnicity (Clewell 1987), international origin (Boyer and Sedlacek 1987), physical impairments (Scherer et al. 1987), and special intracampus demographic groups, for example, transfer students (Boyd 1987) and athletes (Ender 1983). Descriptors of high-risk students also include socioeconomic characteristics. Socioeconomic status is directly correlated with persistence and inversely related to risk (Schaffer 1981). Thus, family background (Eddings 1982), family income (Baylor 1982), and parental education (Coulson et al. 1981) are all socioeconomic variables that contour risk and attrition. Numerous intercorrelations exist, of course, across these variables.

While attrition does occur among students of sound academic standing, the major "cause" of attrition is academic underpreparedness for college (Astin 1975). And while innate abilities and other factors beyond the limits of intervention can lead to academic underpreparedness, a number of other variables appear to be of equal or greater importance. The literature has fully documented the role of psychosocial variables, such as clear-cut goals and self-concept (Pantages and Creedon 1978). The impact of systemic factors has been underemphasized, however.

Academic background and preparation are determinants of academic preparedness. Academic background and preparation, however, in part are socially determined (Reyes and Stanic 1985). Experiences at primary and secondary schools are key determinants of collegiate preparation. Administrative practices like tracking (Raze 1984) may hinder students' preparation for college.

Other psychosocial processes can also contribute to academic underpreparedness. Inefficient instructional approaches (Csikszentmihaly and McCormack 1986) and failure to match instructional styles and cognitive styles (Witkin et al. 1977) can lead to academic underpreparedness among some demographic or socioeconomic populations.

Academic and related factors are compounded by an array of nonacademic factors that increase risk and attrition. Much of the existing literature identifies factors, such as numbers of hours worked, nature and number of credits carried, involvement in extracurricular activities, and similar variables. This study, however, chose to focus on systemic forces that can shape and mold individuals' behavior, thereby reducing the affected parties' capacities to cope. Thus, teachers' negative attitudes, negative self-concept, ethnocentrism, and the operation of a race-/gender-/class-based ontology are introduced as variables shaping risk.

Colleges and universities have directed many of their efforts to combat risk and attrition toward the academic arena. An overwhelming majority of colleges and universities that accept high-risk students also offer courses in basic skills. Numerous institutions, however, have expanded beyond the basics. Comprehensive strategies to build study skills, reinforce academic programs, and provide social support are now offered. Additionally, an increasing number of colleges and universities are beginning to direct efforts toward improving teachers' attitudes toward high-risk students and the efficiency of instruction.

Colleges and universities are also beginning to acknowledge the link between risk at college and students' experiences at primary and secondary schools. Thus, high schools, colleges, and the business community are collaborating to intervene in the broader arena where risk behaviors are cultivated and bred. The future for high-risk students can be optimistic if these measures are pursued.

Ultimately, however, the goal of persistence must become the student's own goal.

Implications for Practice

This monograph emphasizes various factors leading to attrition, focusing on the relationship between systemic and behavioristic variables and framing the elements that are the causes and correlates of risk as being so multifaceted that concerned individuals, groups, and organizations outside of institutions of higher education can, if they choose, play some role in ameliorating risk.

• What can high-risk students do to reduce their own risk?

  1. Perhaps the most damaging role a change agent can play is to formulate the problem of an individual or group

within a framework that denies any element of individual complicity. Students who voluntarily participate in remediation programs show greater improvement in performance than nonvoluntary participants (Boyd 1988). Thus, parents, counselors, advisers, teachers, and peers may be required to "market" the benefits of persistent behaviors to the student. Ultimately, however, the goal of persistence must become the student's own goal.

2. Students must be induced to begin researching information about the labor market and their considered field of study in elementary and secondary school, thus identifying clear-cut goals at an early age. While career development and counseling centers assist college students in this area, present efforts require expansion.

3. Low-achieving college students can participate in tutorials with high school and/or elementary school students. Academic skills of both participants would increase as a consequence of the intervention.

4. High-risk students might wish to seek counseling to improve their ability to cope. Systemic factors create extraordinary stresses. When combined with normal stresses, risk and attrition can result.

• What can the peers of high-risk students do to intervene?

1. Peer counseling, tutorials, and peer advising are formal mechanisms that provide an opportunity for students to assist their high-risk peers.

2. Students can, however, informally and individually assist other students. School clubs and campus organizations can also create their own programs.

3. Students can refrain from displaying negative and/or hostile attitudes toward high-risk students.

• What can teachers do to assist high-risk students?

1. As the literature reveals, teachers have a key role to play. Primary and secondary school systems recognize that teaching skills do not automatically accrue as one acquires degrees in a particular subject. Community colleges too recognize that "good teaching" might involve formal and/ or semiformal training. Many four-year schools with large numbers of high-risk enrollees, however, fail to insist that teachers learn to teach. Teachers can choose, however,

to familiarize themselves with alternative techniques of teaching. They can then use the classroom as a teaching laboratory.

2. Teachers' attitudes are key variables. Teachers of high-risk students must examine their own beliefs regarding minorities, women, socioeconomically disadvantaged students, and other high-risk populations, asking themselves several questions: (1) Do I have built-in biases that tailor my perceptions of the potential of certain students? (2) Do I group students into "good" and "bad"? (3) Do these categories have social, ethnic, and/or class bases? (4) Do I negatively respond to the use of ethnic language and cultural styles? (5) Do I select textbooks that are insulting to various ethnic groups?

3. Teachers who engage students in activities that empower students by permitting the use of their creativity and/or other strengths build self-esteem. Thus, the burden falls on teachers to expand their pedagogies.

4. It is also teachers' responsibility to refer underachieving students to counseling centers.

• What can counselors and academic advisers do to reduce risk and attrition?

1. Intrusive counseling is needed to reduce risk (Lopez et al. 1988).

2. Counseling centers must carefully evaluate the validity and reliability of alternative testing tools so that the needs of high-risk students can be more accurately assessed.

3. Counseling centers could choose to design special orientation programs for foreign students, transfer students, and the disabled.

• What can college administrators do to reduce attrition?

1. College administrators are key. They have the power to implement programs and to mandate participation in them. Academic deans can require faculty to take graduate courses in education.

2. Academic deans can also formally recognize the efforts of teachers who involve themselves with high-risk students by reducing course loads and/or including such work in the guidelines for retaining and promoting faculty.

3. Deans of students can create and staff learning laboratories and/or student learning centers.
4. Administrators can require mandatory advising, which implies the documentation of all advising so that efforts can be evaluated.
5. Administrators can produce and distribute special manuals for students that include a syllabus so that students can ascertain the required amount of work before enrollment.
6. Administrators must work to ensure that marketing efforts to attract high-risk students and the necessary social support systems are complementary.
7. Administrators, particularly deans of students, can include sanctions in the student handbook for incidents involving racially and/or ethnically motivated violence (Jones 1989b).
8. Administrators must ensure that sufficient financial aid is available.

• What can the business community do to reduce risk?

1. Many corporations are creating business and education councils, management personnel "loan" programs, and corporate adopt-a-school programs. More such programs are needed. Indeed, each high school and each college needs a corporate partner.
2. Businesses can play a key role in increasing students' motivation to persist by ensuring that equal opportunities exist for disadvantaged populations upon graduation.
3. Some companies facilitate retention by entering into internship and part-time work agreements with high schools and colleges. More such liaisons are needed.

• What can public policy makers do to reduce risk?

Over recent years, public policy initiatives regarding education have been characterized by anomalies. While various administrators have voiced support for primary, secondary, and higher education, actual and proposed funding has been inconsistent. Indeed, in all but one year of the Reagan administration, the funds the president requested for Pell grants were actually lower than the level appropriated by Congress. In every single year of the Reagan administration, the presidential request for Stafford student loans was below the levels actually appropriated. Such behaviors may have intensified risk and attrition. The following actions are therefore needed for public policy makers.

1. Risk begins during early childhood. The Head Start program, which exists in recognition of this fact, has been effective in ameliorating some of the risks associated with the very young. Thus, policy makers should provide full funding that would serve 100 percent of the eligible population.
2. Public administrators must work to improve coordination between the Head Start and Even Start programs.
3. Attrition could be reduced by federal funding designed to assist institutions of higher education as well as secondary schools in the replication of previously successful programs to reduce attrition. Funding for the retrieval of students who have dropped out would also reduce attrition.
4. Increased federal funding for financial aid rather than loans and targeted funding to historically ethnic colleges and historically female colleges with demonstrated successes in retention would reduce risk.

The Need for Additional Research

Despite the abundance of research on risk and attrition, additional research is needed. First, more meta-analyses are needed so that existing research can be evaluated and assessed. Second, because research regarding risk and attrition is largely atheoretical, empirical research requires careful review as a basis for the development of interdisciplinary models of attrition to systematically integrate systemic and behavioristic elements. Third, survey research is needed regarding the attitudes, beliefs, and opinions of key college personnel regarding high-risk populations. Fourth, the methodologies for assessing the role of specific causal variables need to be refined. Perhaps with new theory and the reevaluation of practice, the magnitude of risk and attrition can soon be reduced.

Several areas for research projects are suggested:

- Experimental designs to test and compare the relative effects of the hypothesized techniques to reduce risk (counseling versus instructional approaches, for example);

- Ongoing monitoring and evaluation of existing programs, techniques, and policies to reduce risk and attrition so that the most successful programs can be replicated;
- Comparative analyses of the effects of micro and macro forces on attrition;
- Comparative analyses of the success or failure of high-risk students at various types of universities (historically black colleges and universities versus predominantly white ones, small versus large, urban versus rural, and so on);
- Longitudinal studies that follow high-risk students from their entrance into institutions of higher education and beyond;
- More intense assessments of the needs of high-risk students to better address both their academic and nonacademic needs.

REFERENCES

The Educational Resources Information Center (ERIC) Clearinghouse
on Higher Education abstracts and indexes the current literature on
higher education for inclusion in ERIC's data base and announce-
ment in ERIC's monthly bibliographic journal, *Resources in Education* (RIE). Most of these publications are available through the
ERIC Document Reproduction Service (EDRS). For publications cited
in this bibliography that are available from EDRS, ordering number
and price code are included. Readers who wish to order a publication should write to the ERIC Document Reproduction Service,
3900 Wheeler Avenue, Alexandria, Virginia 22304. (Phone orders
with VISA or MasterCard are taken at 800/227-ERIC or 703/823-0500.)
When ordering, please specify the document (ED) number. Documents are available as noted in microfiche (MF) and paper copy
(PC). If you have the price code ready when you call EDRS, an exact
price can be quoted. The last page of the latest issue of *Resources
in Education* also has the current cost, listed by code.

Adams, Elaine P., and Bessie S. Smith. 1987. "Factors in Student At-
trition among Students at a Historically Black University." *NASPA
Journal* 24(3): 33–38.
Adams, Howard G. 1988. "Tomorrow's Professorate: Insuring Minority
Participation through Talent Development Today." Paper presented
at the Engineering Dean's Council Student Pipeline Workshop,
American Society for Engineering Education, January, Washington,
D.C. ED 291 273. 10 pp. MF–01; PC–01.
Akbar, N'aim. 1976. "Rhythmic Patterns in African Personality." In
Assumptions and Paradigms for Research on Black People, edited
by L. King et al. Los Angeles: Fanon Center Publications.
American Association for the Advancement of Science. 1984. *Equity
and Excellence: Compatible Goals.* Washington, D.C.: Author, Office
of Opportunities in Science.
Applebee, A.N., J.A. Langer, and I.V.S. Mullis. 1989. *Crossroads in
American Education. A Summary of Findings: The Nation's Report
Card.* Princeton, N.J.: Educational Testing Service.
Arfken, Deborah. 1981. "A Lamp beside the Academic Door: A Look
at the New Student and His Needs." ED 261 603. 17 pp. MF–01;
PC–01.
Arrington, Michael, and John L. Romano. 1980. "Activist Counseling
for Academically Underprepared University Students." ED 193 984.
17 pp. MF–01; PC–01.
Astin, Alexander W. 1975. *Preventing Students from Dropping Out.*
San Francisco: Jossey-Bass.
Bailey, Anne Lowry. 1988. "Corporations Starting to Make Grants to
Public Schools, Diverting Some Funds Once Earmarked for Col-
leges." *Chronicle of Higher Education* 34(22): 28–30.
Banich, Mary Anne. 1988. "The Proper Perspective: Orientation in
the Long Term." *Campus Activities Programming* 21(1): 32–38.

Banks, W.C., G.V. McQuater, and J.L. Hubbard. 1978. "Toward a Re-conceptualization of the Social Cognitive Bases of Achievement Orientations in Blacks." *Review of Educational Research* 48: 381–97.

Baylor, Tondelaya Kateri. 1982. "Equal Education Opportunity Program Clientele: Characteristics, Needs, and Interests." Occasional Paper No. 1. Mansfield, Pa.: Mansfield State College, Department of Special Programs and Learning Resource Center. ED 235 715. 27 pp. MF–01; PC–02.

Beane, D.B. 1985. *Mathematics and Science: Critical Filters for the Future of Minority Students.* Washington, D.C.: American Univ., Mid-Atlantic Center for Race Equity.

Belcher, Marcia J. 1987. *Addressing Retention through an Orientation Course: Results from a North Campus Study.* Research Report No. 87–24. Miami: Miami-Dade Community College, Office of Institutional Research. ED 296 761. 32 pp. MF–01; PC–02.

Bell, D.P. 1974. "Some Characteristics of High- and Low-achieving Seventh Grade Black Students in Mathematics." Ph.D. dissertation, Univ. of Texas at Austin.

Bender, Louis W., and Cheryl D. Blanco. 1987. *Programs to Enhance Participation, Retention, and Success of Minority Students at Florida Community Colleges and Universities.* Research Report. Tallahassee: Florida State Univ., State and Regional Higher Education Center. ED 288 582. 69 pp. MF–01; PC–03.

Bledsoe, Joseph, and Curtis Dixon. 1980. "Effects of Economic Disadvantage on Self-concepts of Urban Black High School Students." *Journal of Psychology* 106(1): 121–27.

Borsi, Emilia, and Fay R. Rogg. 1986. "Teaching Practical Writing Skills to Hispanic Students." Proceedings of the Fifth Annual Eastern Michigan Univ. Conference on Languages for Business and the Professions. ED 295 424. 12 pp. MF–01; PC–01.

Boyd, Vivian. 1987. "Diagnostic and Prescriptive Interviews with Transfer Students in Academic Jeopardy." Research Report No. 16–87. College Park: Univ. of Maryland. ED 291 445. 16 pp. MF–01; PC–01.

———. 1988. "Diagnostic and Prescriptive Group Interviews with Commuting Sophomores in Academic Jeopardy." Research Report No. 1–88. College Park: Univ. of Maryland. ED 296 270. 13 pp. MF–01; PC–01.

Boyer, Susan P., and William E. Sedlacek. 1987. "Noncognitive Predictors of Academic Success for International Students: A Longitudinal Study." Research Report No. 1–87. College Park: Univ. of Maryland, Counseling Center.

Boykin, A.W. 1985. "The Triple Quandary and the Schooling of Afro-American Children." In *The School Achievement of Minority Children,* edited by U. Neiss. Hillsdale, N.J.: Erlbaum.

Bromberg, Matthew. 1984. "A Kind of Equal." *Child and Adolescent*

Social Work Journal 1(2): 71–73.

Brown, Duane, Katherine Fulkerson, et al. September 1983. "Self-estimate Ability in Black and White 8th, 10th, and 12th Grade Males and Females." *Vocational Guidance Quarterly* 32: 21–28.

Brown, John A. 1984. "Group Work with Low-income Black Youths." *Social Work with Groups* 7(3): 111–24.

Campbell, P.B. 1986. "What's a Nice Girl like You Doing in a Math Class?" *Phi Delta Kappan* 67: 516–20.

Carpenter, T. 1980. "Research in Cognitive Development." In *Research in Mathematics Education,* edited by R.J. Shumway. Reston, Va.: National Council of Teachers of Mathematics.

Carroll, Dennis. 1987. "The Effects of Grants on College Persistence." *OERI Bulletin.* Washington, D.C.: Center for Education Statistics. ED 280 355. 9 pp. MF–01; PC–01.

Chapman, Bernadine S. 1982. "Academic Retention and Talent Retrieval." Paper presented at an annual convention of the American Personnel and Guidance Association, March 17–20, Detroit, Michigan. ED 221 821. 27 pp. MF–01; PC–02.

Chronicle of Higher Education. 14 June 1989. "Fact File: Student Loan Default Rates at More than 2,600 Institutions": 28–29.

Clagett, Craig A., and Patricia K. Diehl. 1988. "Course Pass Rates in Fall 1987: Enrollment Analysis Report." Research Report. Largo, Md.: Prince Georges Community College. ED 293 592. 25 pp. MF–01; PC–01.

Clewell, Beatriz Chu. Summer 1987. "Effective Institutional Practice for Improving Minority Retention in Higher Education." *Journal of College Admissions* 116: 7–13.

Cohen, A.M., and F.B. Brauer. 1982. *The American Community College.* San Francisco: Jossey-Bass.

Colasanto, D., and L.F. Williams. January/February 1987. "The Changing Dynamics of Race and Class." *Public Opinion* 9: 50–53.

College Entrance Examination Board. 1985. *Equity and Excellence: The Educational Status of Black Americans.* New York: Author.

College Placement Council. 1989. *Salary Survey: A Study of Beginning Offers.* Bethlehem, Pa.: Author.

Collier, Betty J., and W.D. Smith. 1982. "Distributive Injustice: A Psychosocial Process Analysis." *Universal Renaissance* 3(1): 37–40.

Collison, Michele. 11 February 1987. "How Four Predominantly White Colleges Succeed in Retaining Black and Hispanic Students." *Chronicle of Higher Education* 33(22): 31+.

Connell, Charles, and Lynn Gardner. 1982. *Breaking with Tradition: The Advisor as Change Agent.* Pomora, N.J.: National Academic Advising Association. ED 240 903. 122 pp. MF–01; PC–05.

Cope, Robert G. 1978. "Why Students Stay, Why They Leave." In *Reducing the Dropout Rate: First Steps in Starting a Campus Retention Program,* edited by Lee Noel. New Directions for Student Services No. 3. San Francisco: Jossey-Bass.

Cotnam, John D., and Sherrill Ison. 1988. "A Follow-up Study of Non-returning Students." Research Report. Rochester, N.Y.: Monroe Community College, Office of Institutional Advancement. ED 291 435. 17 pp. MF–01; PC–01.

Coulson, John E., et al. 1981. *Evaluation of the Special Services for Disadvantaged Students (SSDS) Program: 1979–80 Academic Year.* Santa Monica, Cal.: System Development Corporation. ED 214 412. 262 pp. MF–01; PC–11.

Covington, M.V. 1985. "Instruction in Problem Solving Planning." In *Blue Prints for Thinking: The Role of Planning Cognitive Development,* edited by S.L. Friedman, E.K. Scholnick, and R.R. Cocking. Cambridge, Mass.: Cambridge Univ. Press.

Cross, Patricia K. 1979. "Looking Ahead: Spotlight on the Learner." Paper presented at the National Conference on Developmental Evaluation, Lexington, Kentucky. ED 177 791 18 pp. MF–01; PC–01.

———. 1983. "Underprepared Learners." *Current Issues in Higher Education.* Washington, D.C.: American Association for Higher Education.

Crosson, Patricia H. 1987. "Environmental Influences on Minority Degree Attainment." Paper presented at an annual meeting of the Association for the Study of Higher Education, November 21–24, Baltimore, Maryland. ED 292 415. 34 pp. MF–01; PC–02.

Csikszentmihalyi, Mihaly, and Jane McCormack. 1986. "The Influence of Teachers." *Phi Delta Kappan* 67(6): 415–19.

Cuyahoga Community College. 1987. "Transfer Student Follow-up Report: A Follow-up of 1979 and 1984 Students Who Transferred from Cuyahoga Community College to Two Area Universities." Research Report. Cleveland, Ohio: Author. ED 279 374. 27 pp. MF–01; PC–02.

Dale, Grady, Jr. 1981. "Educational Psychology in Action: Learning Skills Training with Health Sciences Students." ED 206 215. 7 pp. MF–01; PC–01.

Denman, Mary Edel. 1983. "Reading and the Academic Content Course." *Reading Improvement* 20(4): 267–73.

Diffenbac, John. 1987. "Expert Systems Could Be a Valuable New Tool for Environment Management." *College and University* 62(4): 306–17.

Dolence, Michael G., et al. 1988. "Strategic Enrollment Management and Planning." *Planning for Higher Education* 16(3): 55–74.

Driscoll, Mark. 1982. *Research within Reach: Secondary School Mathematics.* A Research-Guided Response to the Concerns of Educators. ED 225 842. 170 pp. MF–01; PC–07.

Dumphy, Linda, et al. 1987. "Exemplary Retention Strategies for the Freshman Year." In *Increasing Retention: Academic and Student Affairs Administrators in Partnership,* edited by Martha McCinty Stodt and William M. Klepper. New Directions for Higher Education No. 60. San Francisco: Jossey-Bass.

Duncan, Greg J. Fall 1976. "Earnings, Functions, and Nonpecuniary Benefits." *Journal of Human Resources* 11: 462–83.

Dunn, Tom. March 1987. "Connecting with the Disadvantaged." *Vocational Educational Journal* 62: 35–36.

Dunteman, G.H., et al. 1979. *Race and Sex Differences in College Science Program Participation.* Triangle Park, N.C.: Research Triangle Institute.

Eddings, Diane Dixon. 1982. "A Causal Model of the Attrition of Specially Admitted Black Students in Higher Education." Paper presented at an annual meeting of the American Educational Research Association, March 19–23, New York, New York. ED 224 422. 55 pp. MF–01; PC–03.

Educational Testing Service. 1988. *Focus: Minority Students in Higher Education.* Princeton, N.J.: Author.

Ehrhart, Julie Kuhn, and Bernice R. Sandler. 1987. "Looking for More than a Few Good Women in Traditionally Male Fields." Washington, D.C.: Association of American Colleges, Project on the Status and Education of Women. ED 282 476. 25 pp. MF–01; PC–01.

Ellison, Nolen M., et al. 1987. "Access, Excellence, and Student Retention: A Leadership Commitment." Position Paper. Cleveland, Ohio: Cuyahoga Community College. ED 294 623. 35 pp. MF–01; PC–02.

Ender, Steven. 1983. "Assisting High Academic Risk Athletes: Recommendations for the Academic Advisor." *NACADA Journal* 3(2): 1–10.

Evans, George, and John A. Lucas. 1988. *Follow-up Study of Form Students of the Criminal Justice Program.* Paltise, Ill.: William Rainey Harper College, Office of Planning and Research.

Farrow, Earl V. 1980. *Specialized Programs at Livingstone College: Assessment 1, 1977–80.* New Brunswick, N.J.: Rutgers Univ. ED 213 360. 106 pp. MF–01; PC–05.

Fennema, E., and M. Behr. 1980. "Individual Differences and the Learning of Mathematics." In *Research in Mathematics Education,* edited by R.J. Shumway. Reston, Va.: National Council of Teachers of Mathematics.

Fields, Cheryl. 16 September 1987. "Closing the Education Gap for Hispanics: State Aims to Forestay a Divided Society." *Chronicle of Higher Education* 34(3): 1+.

Fischer, Fredrick J. 1987. "Graduation-Contingent Student Aid." *Change* 19(6): 40–47.

Fordyce, Hugh. 1988. "Retention Data Collection: Problems, Uses, and Suggested Methodology." Research Report 12(1). New York: United Negro College Fund. ED 294 493. 7 pp. MF–01; PC–01.

Fuller, M. 1978. "Reasoning for Experimenters." Paper presented at the Frontiers in Education Conference, May, Orlando, Florida.

Fullerton, Howard N., Jr. July 1982. "How Accurate [Were] the 1980

Labor Force Projections?" *Monthly Labor Review* 105: 15–27.

Geary, Patricia. 1988. "Defying the Odds? Academic Success among At-risk Minority Teenagers in an Urban High School." Paper presented at an annual meeting of the American Educational Research Association, April 5–9, New Orleans, Louisiana. ED 296 055. 9 pp. MF–01; PC–01.

Gerald, Debra E., Paul J. Horn, and William J. Hussar. 1989. *Projections of Education Statistics: 1990 to 2000.* Washington, D.C.: U.S. Dept. of Education, National Center for Education Statistics. ED 312 793. 217 pp. MF–01; PC–09.

Goldman, Ruth E. 1981. "The Classroom as Living Room: Using Group Support Systems to Promote Student Retention and Cognitive Growth in Adult Developmental Students." Paper presented at an annual meeting of the American Educational Research Association, April, Los Angeles, California. ED 203 792. 28 pp. MF–01; PC–02.

Gordon, Roosevelt, Jr. 1987. "A Retention and Achievement Program for Nontraditional Black Students." ED 289 409. 22 pp. MF–01; PC–01.

Gosman, Erica J., et al. 1982. "Student Progression and Attrition in College: Does Race Make a Difference?" Paper presented at an annual meeting of the Association for the Study of Higher Education, March 2–3, New York, New York. ED 219 042. 29 pp. MF–01; PC–02.

Graham, Sandra. 1984. "Communicating Sympathy and Anger to Black and White Children: The Cognitive (Attributional) Consequences of Affective Cues." *Journal of Personality and Social Psychology* 47(1): 40–54.

Greene, Connie, et al. 1987. "Student Success Strategies 1987: Access, Assessment, and Intervention." Paper presented at the Northwest Regional Conference of the National Council on Student Development, February 5–6, Gresham, Oregon. ED 288 598. 24 pp. MF–01; PC–01.

Greene, Elizabeth. October 1987. "South Carolina's Gardner: Self-appointed Spokesman for the Longest Educational Minority Freshman." *Chronicle of Higher Education* 34(6): 41–43.

Gresty, Steven A., and Kevin W. Hunt. 1981. "They Do Not Come Back: Lightfield Revisited." Paper presented at an annual forum of the Association for Institutional Research, May 17–20, Minneapolis, Minnesota. ED 205 070. 34 pp. MF–01; PC–02.

Gwartney, James D., and James E. Long. 1978. "The Relative Earnings of Blacks and Other Minorities." *Industrial and Labor Review* 31(3): 336–46.

Gwin, Stanford P., and Jennifer Downey. 1980. "The Effects of Communication Skill Training on High-risk College Students." Paper presented at an annual meeting of the International Communication Association, May 18–23, Acapulco, Mexico. ED 197 396.

47 pp. MF–01; PC–02.

Hale, J. 1982. *Black Children: Their Roots, Culture, and Learning Styles.* Provo, Utah: Brigham Young Univ. Press.

Hammack, Floyd Morgan. 1986. "Large School Systems' Dropout Reports: An Analysis of Definitions, Procedures, and Findings." *Teachers College Record* 87(3): 324–41.

Harding, Ida B. 1980. "Adjunct Classes: Organizing Resources for High-risk Students." Paper presented at an annual meeting of the Plains Regional Conference of the International Reading Association, September 25–27, Bismarck, North Dakota.

Heard, Frank B. 1988a. "An Assessment of the Tennessee Statewide School/College Collaborative for Educational Excellence: The Middle College High School." Ed.D. practicum paper, Nova Univ. ED 294 637. 32 pp. MF–01; PC–02.

————. 1988b. "The Development of a Retention Plan to Mitigate Low Enrollment at Shelby State Community College." Ed.D. practicum paper, Nova Univ. ED 296 751. 43 pp. MF–01; PC–02.

Hechinger, Fred M. 1979. "Basic Skills: Closing the Gap." *Change* 11(7): 28–33.

Hirschorn, Michael W. 1988. "Coalition of 120 Colleges Hope to Encourage a Million Students to Tutor 'At Risk' Youths." *Chronicle of Higher Education* 34(20): 38.

Hixson, Bruce. 1982. "General College Program and Projects Receiving Outside Financial Support." *General College Newsletter* 29(1): 1.

Hodges, Daniel L. 1988. "How to Improve Student Retention: Five Areas of Psychological Research and Their Applications. A Teaching Guide." ED 296 772. 19 pp. MF–01; PC–01.

Holahan, Carole, et al. 1983. "A Six-year Longitudinal Analysis of Transfer Student Performance and Retention." *Journal of College Student Personnel* 24: 305–10.

Holliday, Bertha G. 1985. "Differential Effects of Children's Self-perceptions and Teachers' Perceptions of Black Children's Academic Achievement." *Journal of Negro Education* 54(1): 71–81.

Hossler, Don. 1987. "Enrollment Management: Institutional Application." *College and University* 62(2): 106–16.

Hunziker, Celeste. 1987. "Persistence and Graduating U.C.–Davis Undergraduates Admitted by Special Action: 1975–1985." Research Report. Davis: Univ. of California, Office of Student Affairs. ED 283 469. 16 pp. MF–01; PC–01.

Illinois Community College Board. 1987. "Female Student Participation at Illinois Public Community Colleges." Research Report. Springfield: Author. ED 281 581. 18 pp. MF–01; PC–01.

Jaschik, Scott. July 1987. "State Leaders Urged to Intensify Colleges' Efforts to Enroll and Graduate More Minority Students." *Chronicle of Higher Education* 33(44): 1+.

Jenkins, Jeannette, et al. 1981. *Promoting Persistence through Cog-*

nitive Style Analysis and Self-management Techniques. Carbondale: Southern Illinois Univ., College of Education. ED 222 142. 67 pp. MF–01; PC–03.

Johnson, Naomi J., and Richard C. Richardson, Jr. 1986. "A Causal Model of Academic Factors Affecting Student Persistence." Paper presented at an annual meeting of the American Educational Research Association, April, San Francisco, California. ED 271 075. 29 pp. MF–01; PC–02.

Johnson, S.T. 1988. "Test Fairness and Bias: Measuring Academic Achievement among Black Youth." *Urban League Review* 11(1,2): 76–92.

Johnson, S.T., and S.E. Prom. 1984. *Factors Related to Science and Mathematics Career Choice: A Survey of Alumni of A Better Chance, Inc.* Final Report. New York: Ford Foundation.

Jones, Dionne J. 1987. "Factors Associated with Mathematics Achievement and the Selection of a Mathematics-related or a Nonmathematics-related Major among Black College Students." Ph.D. dissertation, Howard Univ.

———. 1988. "Intellectual Imperialism and Public Policy: The Head Start Program." Paper presented at an annual conference of the American Evaluation Association, October, New Orleans, Louisiana.

———. 1989a. "Against the Odds: The Educational Achievement of African-American Women." Paper presented at an annual meeting of the Association of Social and Behavioral Scientists, March, Atlanta, Georgia.

———. 1989b. *Racially Motivated Violence: An Empirical Study of a Growing Social Problem.* Discussion Paper No. 1. Washington, D.C.: National Urban League, Research Department.

Jones, Dionne J., and Betty J. Watson. 1988. "The Increasing Significance of Race." In *Poverty, Race, and Public Policy,* edited by Billy J. Tidwell. Lanham, Md.: National Urban League Press.

Jones, L.V. 1985. "Black-White Differences in Mathematics: Some New Research Findings." Paper presented at the 69th Annual Meeting of the American Educational Research Association, March/April, Chicago, Illinois. ED 257 637. 13 pp. MF–01; PC–02.

Jones, L.V., N.W. Burton, and E.C. Davenport, Jr. 1984. "Monitoring the Mathematics Achievement of Black Students." *Journal for Research in Mathematics Education* 15(3): 154–64.

Joyce, Corine. 1980. "The Goal Center at Donnelly College." ED 198 778. 6 pp. MF–01; PC–01.

Kaliszeski, Michael S. 1988. "Clark's 'Cooling Out' Concept as a Factor in Student Completion of Community College Programs." Graduate seminar paper, Univ. of Florida. ED 290 512. 15 pp. MF–01; PC–01.

Karabel, Jerome, and Alexander W. Astin. March 1975. "Social Class, Academic Ability, and College 'Quality.'" *Social Forces* 53: 381–91.

Kaufmann, G. 1979. *Visual Imagery and Its Relations to Problem Solving.* New York: Columbia Univ. Press.

Kelly, Kathleen. 1988. "Mount St. Mary's College, Doheny Campus: A Comprehensive Program of Retention for an Ethnically Diverse Student Body." Los Angeles, Cal.: Author. ED 292 503. 7 pp. MF–01; MF–01.

Klausmeier, H., and Associates. 1979. *Cognitive Learning and Development: Piagetian and Information-processing Perspectives.* Cambridge, Mass.: Ballinger.

Klein, James D., and Phillip J. Grise. 1987. "GED and Traditional High School Diploma Holders Attending Florida's Community Colleges: A Comparison of Academic Success." GED Research Brief No. 12. Washington, D.C.: American Council on Education. ED 291 892. 5 pp. MF–01; PC–01.

Kleinschrad, W.A. February 1987. "Where Have All the Workers Gone?" *Administrative Management* 48: 45.

Kovack, M. 1986. "Danger: Worker Shortage Ahead." *Compensation Benefits Review* 18(1): 60–64.

Krajewski, Robert J., and Barbara J. Simmons. 1988. "The Role of Colleges of Education in the Recruitment and Retention of Minorities." *Teacher Education and Practice* 4(1): 53–56.

Kuh, George D., and Elizabeth J. Whitt. 1988. *The Invisible Tapestry: Culture in American Colleges and Universities.* ASHE-ERIC Higher Education Report No. 1. Washington, D.C.: Association for the Study of Higher Education.

Kulik, Chen-Lin, James A. Kulik, and Barbara J. Shwalb. 1983. "College Programs for High-Risk and Disadvantaged Students: A Meta-analysis of Findings." *Review of Educational Research* 53(3): 397–414.

Lavin, David E., et al. 1983. "Socioeconomic Origins and Educational Background of an Entering Class at CUNY: A Comparison of Regular and Special Program Enrollees. Fall 1980 Freshman Cohort Study." Report No. 1. New York: City Univ. of New York, Office of Institutional Research and Analysis. ED 234 701. 60 pp. MF–01; PC–03.

Lee, Beth S. 1987. "Measures of Progress: 1984–1987. A Four-year Retrospective." Research Report. Sacramento, Cal.: Los Rios Community College District, Office of Planning and Research. ED 293 580. 68 pp. MF–01; PC–03.

Lenning, Oscar T., Phillip E. Beal, and Ken Sauer. 1980. *Retention and Attrition: Evidence for Action and Research.* Boulder, Colo.: National Center for Higher Education Management Systems. ED 192 661. 134 pp. MF–01; PC–06.

Lifschutz, Ellen. December 1982. "Special Sections of Freshman English: Pragmatic Approach to Teaching." *University Students with Poor Writing Skills.* ED 247 574. 22 pp. MF–01; PC–01.

Lopez, Mike, et al. 1988. "Intrusive Advising with Special Student

Populations." *NASPA Journal* 25(3): 195–201.

Losak, John, et al. Fall 1982. "College Students in Remedial Courses Report on Their High School Preparation." *College Board Review* 125: 21–22+.

Ludwig, L. Mark. 1977. "Educational Consulting Study: Special Techniques for Assisting the Underprepared College Student." Working Papers on Professional Development in Teaching No. 5. Cleveland: Cleveland Commission on Higher Education. ED 175 324. 31 pp. MF–01; PC–02.

Lum, Glen, and Richard Alfred. 1987. "Remedial Program Policies, Student Demographic Characteristics, and Performance Outcomes in Community Colleges." Paper presented at an annual meeting of the Association for the Study of Higher Education, February 13–17, San Diego, California. ED 281 452. 90 pp. MF–01; PC–04.

Luxenberg, Stan. 1977. "The College Takes a High School." *Change* 9(12): 21–23.

McCarthy, Patricia, and Scott Meir. 1983. "Effects of Race and Psychological Variables on College Student Writing." *Journal of Instructional Psychology* 10(3): 148–57.

McDade, Laurie A. 1988. "Knowing the 'Right Stuff': Attrition, Gender, and Scientific Literacy." *Anthropology and Education Quarterly* 19(2): 93–114.

McPhail, Irving P. 1978. "University Faculty Institute Emphasizes Basic Skills in the Content Areas." ED 193 695. 12 pp. MF–01; PC–01.

Madhere, Serge. 1989. "Models of Intelligence and the Black Intellect." *Journal of Negro Education* 58(2): 189–202.

Maestas-Flores, Margarita, and Mauro Chavez. 1987. *Puente Project: The Mentor's Guide.* San Jose, Cal.: Evergreen Valley College. ED 289 551. 46 pp. MF–01; PC–02.

Marrett, C.B. 1981. *Patterns of Enrollment in High School Mathematics and Science.* Final Report. Madison: Wisconsin Research and Development Center.

Marrett, C.B., and H. Gates. 1983. "Male-Female Enrollment across Mathematics Tracks in Predominantly Black High Schools." *Journal for Research in Mathematics Education* 14(2): 113–18.

Martin, William J. 1987. "New Student Intake: A Retention Model for Community Colleges." *NASPA Journal* 24(4): 12–22.

Matthews, W., T.P. Carpenter, M.M. Lindquist, and E.A. Silver. 1984. "The Third National Assessment: Minorities and Mathematics." *Journal for Research in Mathematics Education* 15(3): 165–71.

Mendoza, Jose, and Carl Samuels. 1987. *Faculty Mentoring System for Minority Student Retention.* Year-end Report, 1986–87. Glendale, Ariz.: Glendale Community College. ED 288 588. 38 pp. MF–01; PC–02.

Metzner, Barbara S., and John P. Blair. 1987. "The Estimation of a Conceptual Model of Nontraditional Undergraduate Student Attrition." *Research in Higher Education* 27(1): 15–38.

Mitchell, Tom. 1987. "Preparing the Unprepared: Revising LJC's Remedial Program." Laredo, Tex.: Laredo Junior College.

Mitchem, Arnold L. 23 June 1982. "Testimony to the National Commission on Excellence in Education." Public Hearing. Chicago: Author. ED 227 094. 10 pp. MF–01; PC–01.

Moen, Norman W. 1980. "Renovation of the A.A. Degree Program: The General College Retention (PEP) Program Evaluation of General College." *General College Newsletter* 26(3): 1. ED 190 976. 26 pp. MF–01; PC–02.

Moline, Arlett E. 1987. "Financial Aid and Student Persistence: An Application of Causal Modeling." *Research in Higher Education* 26(2): 130–47.

Moore, Kristin A. September 1989. "Facts at a Glance." Washington, D.C.: Child Trends, Inc.

Mullis, Ina V.S., and Lynn B. Jenkins. 1988. *The Science Report Card: Elements of Risk and Recovery.* National Assessment of Educational Progress. Princeton, N.J.: Educational Testing Service.

Murdock, Tullisse A. 1987. "It Isn't Just Money: The Effects of Financial Aid on Student Persistence." *Review of Higher Education* 7(1): 75–101.

National Coalition of Advocates for Students. 1985. *Barriers to Excellence: Our Children at Risk.* Boston: Author.

Newton, Eunice Shaed. 1982. *The Case for Improved College Teaching: Instructing High-risk College Students.* New York: Vantage Press.

Nisbet, Janice. 1982. "Predictors of Academic Success with High-risk College Students." *Journal of College Student Personnel* 23(3): 227–387.

Noel, Lee, ed. 1978. *Reducing the Dropout Rate: First Steps in Starting a Campus Retention Program.* New Directions for Student Services No. 3. San Francisco: Jossey-Bass.

Olstad, A., J. Juarez, L. Davenport, and D. Harry. 1981. *Inhibitors to Achievement in Science and Mathematics by Ethnic Minorities.* ED 223 404. 136 pp. MF–01; PC–06.

Pantages, Timothy J., and Carol F. Creedon. 1978. "Studies of College Attrition: 1950–1975." *Review of Educational Research* 48(1): 49–101.

Pascarella, Ernest T., and Patrick T. Terenzini. 1975. "Informal Interaction with Faculty and Freshman Ratings of the Academic and Nonacademic Experience of College." Syracuse, N.Y.: Univ. of Syracuse. ED 165 593. 27 pp. MF–01; PC–02.

Pawlicki, Lynn, and Charles Connell. 1981. *NACADA Journal* 1(1): 44–52.

Payne, Jarize. 1987. "My Experience with the Peer Mentor Program." *Children Today* 16(4): 20.

Pettigrew, Thomas, et al. 1982. *Prejudice.* Cambridge, Mass.: Belknap Press/Harvard Univ. Press.

Phillips, Deborah, and Edward Zigler. 1980. "Children's Self-image Disparity: Effects of Age, Socioeconomic Status, Ethnicity, and Gender." *Journal of Personality and Social Psychology* 39(4): 689–700.

Pinkston, Ria R. 1987. "University Support Programs, Academic Achievement, and Retention." ED 283 441. 11 pp. MF–01; PC–01.

Pittman, Karen, and Gina Adams. 1988. *Teenage Pregnancy: An Advocate's Guide to the Numbers.* Washington, D.C.: Children's Defense Fund.

Polson, P.G., and R. Jeffries. 1985. "Analysis-Instruction in General Problem Solving Skills: An Analysis of Four Approaches." In *Thinking and Learning Skills.* Vol. 1, Relating Instruction to Research, edited by J.W. Segal, S.F. Chipman, and R. Glaser. Hillside, N.J.: Erlbaum.

Prom, S.E. 1982. "Salient Content and Cognitive Performance of Person- and Thing-oriented Low-income Afro-American Children in Kindergarten and Second Grade." Ph.D. dissertation, Howard Univ.

Pruitt, Anne S. 1979. "Stop the Revolving Door." *AGB Reports* 21(2): 17–19.

Puyear, Don, ed. 1987a. *Exemplary Marketing and Retention Practices in the Virginia Community College System.* Vol. 2. Richmond: Virginia Dept. of Community Colleges. ED 283 559. 287 pp. MF–01; PC–12.

———. 1987b. *The "Ins and Outs" of Marketing and Retention in Virginia's Community Colleges.* Vol. 1. Richmond: Virginia Dept. of Community Colleges. ED 283 558. 27 pp. MF–01; PC–02.

Radcliffe, Susan, and Cheryl Baxter. 1984. *Follow-up of 1982 Graduates.* Research Report. Columbia, Md.: Howard Community College, Office of Institutional Research.

Ramirez, M., III, and A. Castenada. 1974. *Cultural Democracy, Bicognitive Development, and Education.* New York: Academic Press.

Raze, N. 1984. "Overview of Research on Ability Grouping." Redwood City, Cal.: San Mateo County Office of Education. ED 252 927. 11 pp. MF–01; PC–01.

Reed, Sherry. 1982. *TRIO/Special Services Program Evaluation.* Final Report 1981–82. Minneapolis: Univ. of Minnesota, General College. ED 224 418. 145 pp. MF–01; PC–06.

Reed, Suellen B., and Nancy C. Hudepohl. 1983. "High-risk Nursing Students: Emergence of Remedial/Development Programs." *Nurse Educator* 8(4): 21–26.

Resnick, D.P., and L.B. Resnick. 1985. "Standards, Curriculum, and Performance: A Historical and Comparative Perspective." *Educational Researcher* 14(4): 5–21.

Resnick, Lauren B. 1986. *Education and Learning to Think.* Special Report. Pittsburgh: Univ. of Pittsburgh, Commission on Behavioral and Social Sciences and Education.

Reyes, L.H., and G.M.A. Stanic. 1985. "A Review of Literature on Blacks and Mathematics." Paper presented at an annual meeting of the American Educational Research Association, April, Chicago, Illinois.

Richardson, Richard C., Jr. 1983. "Open Access and Institutional Policy: Time for Reexamination." *College Review* 10(4): 47–51.

Richardson, Richard C., Jr., and Alfred G. De Los Santos, Jr. 1988. "From Access to Achievement: Fulfilling the Promise." *Review of Higher Education* 7(4): 323–28.

Riles, Wilson. 1980. "The Underprepared Student: A Problem for Solving." *AGB Reports* 22(6): 17–20.

Roberts, Veronica A. 1989. "An Evaluation of Secondary School Mathematics: Relationships among Instructional Equality, Teacher Certification, and Student Achievement Test Scores." Paper presented at an annual conference of the American Educational Research Association, March, San Francisco, California.

———. 1990. "Relationships among Processing Behavior Mode, Cognitive Development Level, and Mathematics Achievement in Black Metropolitan High School Students." Ph.D. dissertation, Howard Univ.

Roderich, G.W., and J.M. Bell. 1981. "Unqualified Mature Students at the University of Sheffield." *Studies in Higher Education* 6(2): 123–29.

Romberg, T.A., and F. Tufte. 1986. *Mathematics Curriculum for Engineering: Some Suggestions from Cognitive Science.* Madison, Wis.: School Mathematics Monitoring Center.

Ross, David B. 1987. "Students Who Drop Out before They Begin: A Study of Potential Community College Students Who Initiate the Registration Process but Fail to Enroll." *Community Junior College Quarterly of Research and Practice* 11(2): 93–101.

Schaffer, Garnett Stokes. 1981. "Use of a Biographical Questionnaire in the Early Identification of College Dropouts." Paper presented at an annual meeting of the Southeastern Psychological Association, Atlanta, Georgia. ED 208 288. 14 pp. MF–01; PC–01.

Scherer, Marcia J., et al. 1987. "Factors Affecting Persistence of Deaf College Students." Paper presented at an annual meeting of the American Educational Research Association, April 20–24, Washington, D.C. ED 291 187. 35 pp. MF–01; PC–02.

Schmedinghoff, Gerard J. 1979. "A College Program for High-risk Students." *College and University* 55(1): 64–78.

Schoenberger, Ann K. 1988. "College Women's Persistence in Engineering and Physical Science: A Further Study." Paper presented at an annual meeting of the American Educational Research Association, April 5–9, New Orleans, Louisiana. ED 296 889. 47 pp. MF–01; PC–02.

Semerod, R.D. 9 February 1987. "2000: Labor Shortage Looms." *Industry Week* 232: 38–40.

Sentelle, Sam P. 1980. "A Helping Hand for the Chronic Truant." *Ed-*

ucational Leadership 37(6): 471–72.

Shade, B.J. 1984. "Afro-American Patterns of Cognition: A Review of Research." Paper presented at an annual meeting of the American Educational Research Association, April, New Orleans, Louisiana. ED 244 025. 29 pp. MF–01; PC not available EDRS.

Sharkey, Stuart J., et al. 1987. "Pioneer Program for Retraining 'At-risk' Students." New Directions for Higher Education No. 4. San Francisco: Jossey-Bass.

Sheridan, E. Marcia. 1982. *Sex Stereotypes and Reading: Research and Strategies.* Newark, Del: International Reading Association. ED 211 970. 129 pp. MF–01; PC–06.

Sidel, Celia, and Marie McCullough. 1980. "Personal Development and Comprehensive Support Services." Knoxville: Univ. of Tennessee.

Skinner, Elizabeth Fisk, and Richard C. Richardson. 1988. "Making It in a Majority University: The Minority Graduate's Perspective." *Change* 20(3): 34–42.

Smith, Jackie. 1987. "Reflections of a Peer Mentor." *Children Today* 16(4): 21.

Smurthwaite, Ann. 1977. "A Report on the Early Leavers Scheme at Monash University." ED 165 507. 77 pp. MF–01; PC–04.

Sollimo, Vincent J. 1988. *A Retention Study at Burlington County College in General College Chemistry.* Pemberton, N.J.: Burlington College.

Spady, W. 1970. "Dropouts from Higher Education: An Interdisciplinary Review and Synthesis," *Interchange* 1(1): 64–65.

Spann, Milton G., Jr. 1977. "Building a Developmental Education Program." In *Increasing Basic Skills by Developmental Studies,* edited by John E. Roueche. New Directions for Higher Education No. 20. San Francisco: Jossey-Bass.

Spence, Charles C. 1988. "Enrollment Management: A Key to Student Success." Paper presented at an annual convention of the American Association of Community and Junior Colleges, April, Las Vegas, Nevada. ED 294 636. 38 pp. MF–01; PC–02.

Starks, Gretchen. 1987. "Retention of Adult Women Students in the Community College: Research Findings from Exceptional Case Studies." Paper presented at an annual meeting of the American Educational Research Association, April 20–24, Washington, D.C. ED 281 592. 13 pp. MF–01; PC–01.

State Higher Education Executive Officers Association. 1987. *A Difference of Degrees: State Initiatives to Improve Minority Student Achievement.* Report and Recommendations of the Task Force on Minority Student Achievement. Denver: Author. ED 287 355. 75 pp. MF–01; PC–03.

Steere, Marcia. 1984. "The Black/White Dichotomy and the Classroom." *Journal of Creative Behavior* 18(4): 247–55.

Thoren, Daniel. 1987. "Reducing Class Size at the Community College." Princeton, N.J.: Princeton Univ., Mid-Career Fellowship Program.

Tidwell, Romeria. 1980. "Gifted Students' Self-images as a Function of Identification Procedure, Race, and Sex." *Journal of Pediatric Psychology* 5(1): 57–69.

Tinto, Vincent. 1975. "Dropouts from Higher Education: A Theoretical Synthesis of Recent Research." *Review of Educational Research* 45(1): 89–125.

———. 1987. *Leaving College: Rethinking the Causes and Cures of Student Attrition.* Chicago: Univ. of Chicago Press. ED 283 416. 246 pp. MF–01; PC–10.

Tom, Alice K. 1982. "Nontraditional Predictors of Academic Success for Special Action Admissions." Davis: Univ. of California at Davis, Office of Student Affairs. ED 256 268. 35 pp. MF–01; PC–02.

Tuck, Kathy D. 1988. *A Study of Students Who Left: D.C. Public School Dropouts.* Washington, D.C.: District of Columbia Public Schools.

U.S. Congress. 1988. *Staff Report on the Guaranteed Student Loan Program: Belmont Task Force Recommendations.* Prepared for the Subcommittee on Postsecondary Education of the House Committee on Education and Labor. Washington, D.C.: U.S. Government Printing Office.

U.S. Department of Commerce, Bureau of the Census. 1989. *Statistical Abstract of the United States, 1989.* Washington, D.C.: U.S. Government Printing Office.

U.S. Department of Education, National Center for Education Statistics. 1981. *High School and Beyond: A National Longitudinal Study for the 1980s.* Washington, D.C.: U.S. Government Printing Office. ED 214 990. 261 pp. MF–01; PC–11.

———. 1987. "School Dropouts in the United States." Issue Paper. Washington, D.C.: U.S. Government Printing Office.

———. 1988. *Digest of Education Statistics, 1988.* Washington, D.C.: U.S. Government Printing Office.

———. 1989. *Digest of Education Statistics, 1989.* Washington, D.C.: U.S. Government Printing Office. ED 312 792. 542 pp. MF–02; PC–22.

U.S. Department of Justice. 1987. *Crime in the United States, 1986.* Uniform Crime Reports. Washington, D.C.: Federal Bureau of Investigation.

U.S. Department of Labor, Bureau of Labor Statistics. 25 June 1987. "BLS Previews the Economy of the Year 2000." News Release. Washington, D.C.: U.S. Government Printing Office.

———. 1988. *Employment and Earnings.* Washington, D.C.: U.S. Government Printing Office.

Valencia Community College. 1987. "REACH: Resources Education Achievement Challenge and Hope Program." 1986–1987 Final Report. Orlando, Fla: Author. ED 287 539. 36 pp. MF–01; PC–02.

Van Allen, Georgio N. 1988. "Retention! A Commitment to Student

Achievement." *Journal of College Student Development* 29(2): 163–65.

Vance, H., and A. Engin. 1978. "Analysis of Cognitive Abilities of Black Children's Performance on WISC-R." *Journal of Clinical Psychology* 34: 452–56.

Vaz, Kim. 1987. "Building Retention Systems for Talented Minority Students Attending White Universities." *Negro Educational Review* 38(1): 23–29.

Vincent, Vern C. 1983. "Impact of a College Learning Assistance Center on the Achievement and Retention of Disadvantaged Students." ED 283 438. 15 pp. MF–01; PC–01.

Wagner, S. 1977. "Conservation of Equation and Function and Its Relationship to Formal Operational Thought." Paper presented at an annual meeting of the American Educational Research Association, April 4–8, New York, New York. ED 141 117. 28 pp. MF–01; PC–02.

Walleri, R. Dan. 1987. "A Longitudinal Study of 'Guided Studies' Students." Paper presented at an annual forum of the Association for Institutional Research, May 3–6, Kansas City, Missouri. ED 293 432. 22 pp. MF–01; PC–01.

Walters, David. 1987. "The Take Advantage Now/Parent Education Project." *Linkages: Perspectives from Special Programs* 5(1): 3–8. ED 296 022. 7 pp. MF–01; PC–01.

Warming, Eloise D. 1980. "Aids for High-risk Students to Become Efficient Readers and Persistent Learners: Effective Teaching Methods and Materials." Paper presented at an annual meeting of the International Reading Association, St. Louis, Missouri. ED 190 989. 22 pp. MF–01; PC not available EDRS.

Warner, W. Lloyd, and Leo Strole. 1945. *The Social Systems of American Ethnic Groups.* New Haven, Conn.: Yale Univ. Press.

Washington Post. 1 February 1989. "Survey of Math, Science Skills Puts U.S. Students at Bottom."

Watson, Betty. 1987. "Is the Labor Market Color-Blind?" In *Quarterly Report on the Black Worker,* edited by Monica L. Jackson. Washington, D.C.: National Urban League, Research Department.

Watson, Betty, and Cyprian Rowe. *In press. Demythologizing Poverty.* Washington, D.C.: Howard Univ. Press.

Watson, Betty, and W. Smith. 1987. "Understanding the Current Debate over Public Policy." *Phylon* 48(1): 14–17.

Webb, Edward M. 1987. "Retention and Excellence through Student Involvement: A Leadership Role for Student Affairs." *NASPA Journal* 24(4): 6–11.

Whimbey, A., and J. Lochhead. 1984. *Beyond Problem Solving and Comprehension.* Philadelphia: Franklin Institute Press.

Wilbur, Franklin P. 1988. *School-College Partnerships: A Look at the Major National Models.* Washington, D.C.: American Association for Higher Education.

Wilson, R., and D.J. Carter. 1988. *Minorities in Higher Education.* Seventh Annual Status Report. Washington D.C.: American Council on Education, Office of Minority Concerns.

Witkin, H.A., and D.R. Goodenough. 1981. *Cognitive Styles: Essence and Origins.* New York: International Universities Press.

Witkin, H.A., C.A. Moore, D.R. Goodenough, and P.W. Cox. 1977. "Field-dependent and Field-independent Cognitive Styles and Their Educational Implications." *Review of Education Research* 47(1): 1–64.

Woodward, Chris. 1988. "The Effects of Single-year Scholarships versus Renewable Scholarships on Student Persistence." *College and University* 63(2): 162–67.

Wooldridge, Horace W., Jr. 1982. "The Developmental Student: Advising Challenges of the 1980s." *NACADA Journal* 2(1): 8–12.

Yamagishi, Midori, and Gerald M. Gillmore. 1980. "The Relationship between Nelson-Denny Test Scores and Academic Performance of Educational Opportunity Program Students." Seattle: Washington Univ., Educational Assessment Center. ED 197 656. 30 pp. MF–01; PC–02.

Zuckerman, Diane. 1980. "Self-esteem, Self-concept, and the Life Goals and Sex-Role Attitudes of College Students." *Journal of Personality* 48(2): 149–62.

INDEX

A

Abstract concepts, 41
Academic achievement, 52
Academic background, 84
Academic curricula, 22
Academic
        preparedness, 84
        reinforcement, 76
        support services, 74
        underpreparedness, 34, 47, 84
Access to academic resources, 35
Activist counseling, 78
Administrators, 77
Adult students, 84
Advisors and counselors, 77
Affective behavior, 60
African-American students, 16
Analytical thinking, 42
Aspirations African-Americans, 51
Assimilation, 58
Athletes, 12
Attrition, 1, 33, 67, 83
        and gender, 11
        and race, 11
        rates: African-Americans, 31
        effects on funding, 22
        high school students, 63

B

Boston College, 71
Brooklyn College, 78
Bureau of Labor Statistics, 27

C

California State University
        at Fresno, 71
        at Los Angeles, 70
Class-based ontology, 56
Cognitive
        development, 39
        factors: students, 41
        problem solving, 42
College
        enrollment of African-Americans, 31
        participation rates, 50
Colleges and universities: expenditures, 4
Competitiveness and attrition, 31

Computer use: college students, 30-31
Concrete learning, 41
Costs: educational institutions, 22
Cue selection: African-Americans, 43

D

Demographic variables, 14
Developmental levels: students, 40
Disadvantaged
     children, 33
     groups, 7
Doctoral degrees: African-Americans, 51
Donnelly College, 25
Dropout rates, 61

E

Economy: United States, 31
Educational expenditures, 4
Educational Testing Service, 47
Enhancement of self-esteem, 74
Enrollment changes, 23
Environmental variables, 14
Ethnocentric behavior, 58
Ethnocentrism, 57-59
Ethnocultural differences: teacher attitudes, 57
Eurocentrism, 57-59
Evergreen Valley College, 79
Expenditures: public schools, 35

F

Facilities planning, 24
Faculty interventions, 78
Family support, 78
Field dependence, 42-43
Financial
     aid and persistence, 17
     assistance, 24
     support, 79
Flexible admission standards, 5
Florida: community colleges and universities, 5
Foreign student enrollment, 14
Funding patterns, 22
Future
     labor force characteristics, 27
     labor market: high-risk students, 27

G

Gender-based ontology, 56
Glendale Community College, 79

Grade point averages, 8
Grambling State University, 75
Gross national product projections, 28

H

Head Start, 33
Hearing-impaired students, 14
High-risk students and society, 21
High-risk students
 demographics, 10
 profiles and characteristics, 3
 recruitment, 72
 socioeconomic characteristics, 15
Holism, 41-45

I

Identifying high-risk students, 68
Implications for the future, 85-90
Impulsivity, 43
Income
 of nonpersisters, 21
 of persisters, 21
Indiana University, 71
Information processing
 African-Americans, 43
 students, 39
 styles, 41
Institutional commitment, 69
Instructional styles, 46
Intellect: structure of, 45
International students, 13
Invisible tapestry, 3

J

Juvenile delinquency, 64

L

Labor force
 demographic composition, 28
 twenty-first century, 28
Labor market
 projections, 28
 preparedness, 30
Labor shortage, 28
Level of risk, 83
Loan default, 80
Low self-esteem, 59

M

Manhattan Community College, 76
Mansfield State College, 16
Mathematical ability, 45
Mathematics
    and minority students, 37-38
    proficiency of African-Americans, 47, 49
    proficiency of whites, 47, 49
Mechanisms of attrition, 55, 56
Median income: African-American families, 16
Meta analyses, 89
Miami-Dade Community College, 75
Minorities: educational achievement, 5, 6
Mount St. Mary's College, 70

N

National Assessment of Educational Progress, 47
National Collegiate Athletic Association, 12
Negative attitudes: teachers, 56
Nelson-Denny reading test, 13
Nonacademic courses, 25
Nontraditional
    students, 4, 84
    students characteristics, 9, 84

O

One-parent households, 62
Opportunity, equality of, 4
Oregon community colleges, 70
Orientation courses, 75
Outreach, 71

P

Parental education and risk, 17
Parental occupation and risk, 17
Pell grants, 80
Piaget, 39
Preschool programs and high-risk students, 33
Psychodynamics of systemic forces, 59
Purdue University, 71

R

Race-based ontology, 56
Reading proficiency
    African-Americans, 47
    whites, 47
Reduction of attrition: strategies, 67-68
Regular admits, 7

Reinforcing academic skills, 76
Remedial courses, 25, 75
Retention
        institutional support, 69
        programs, 68-71
        rates: graduate students, 50, 51
Revenues
        higher education, 23
Risk, 1, 67, 83
Risk and attrition: nonacademic factors, 55

S

San Diego State University, 76
Scholastic Aptitude Test
        African-Americans, 49, 50
        scores, 12
Science proficiency
        African-Americans, 48
        whites, 48
Selectivity, 43
Self-fulfilling prophecy, 61
Shelby State Community College, 11, 25
Social
        dynamics of attrition, 61
        mobility, 4
        stratification, 55
        support, 77
Socioeconomic status, 15
Southern Illinois University, 73
Southwest Texas State University, 13
Special admits, 7
State Higher Education Executive Officers Association (SHEEO), 8
Structure of American society, 58
Student profile, 9
Students helping students, 79

T

Teacher attitudes and ethnocultural differences in students, 57
Teaching higher-order skills, 46
Teenage pregnancy, 61-62
"Tracking", 35-38
Training: labor force, 27
Transfer students, 13
Truancy, 62

U

Unemployment
> African-Americans, 29
> Hispanics, 29
> whites, 29

University
> of California at Davis, 5
> of Maryland, 13, 73
> of Massachusetts, 10
> of Minnesota, 25, 74
> of North Carolina at Greensboro, 71
> of Sheffield, 10
> of Tennessee, 74

V

Valencia Community College, 76
Value of education, 52
Virginia community college system, 68

W

Washington community colleges, 70
Wayne Community College, 71
William Rainey Harper College, 74
Writing performance
> African-Americans, 47
> whites, 47

X

Xenophobia, 57

ASHE-ERIC HIGHER EDUCATION REPORTS

Since 1983, the Association for the Study of Higher Education (ASHE) and the Educational Resources Information Center (ERIC) Clearinghouse on Higher Education, a sponsored project of the School of Education and Human Development at The George Washington University, have cosponsored the *ASHE-ERIC Higher Education Report* series. The 1990 series is the nineteenth overall and the second to be published by the School of Education and Human Development at the George Washington University.

Each monograph is the definitive analysis of a tough higher education problem, based on thorough research of pertinent literature and insitutional experiences. Topics are identified by a national survey. Noted practitioners and scholars are then commissioned to write the reports, with experts providing critical reviews of each manuscript before publication.

Eight monographs (10 before 1985) in the ASHE-ERIC Higher Education Report series are published each year and are available on individual and subscription basis. Subscription to eight issues is $80.00 annually; $60 to members of AAHE, AIR, or AERA; and $50 to ASHE members. All foreign subscribers must include an additional $10 per series year for postage.

To order single copies of existing reports, use the order form on the last page of this book. Regular prices, and special rates available to members of AAHE, AIR, AERA and ASHE, are as follows:

Series	Regular	Members
1990	$17.00	$12.75
1988-89	15.00	11.25
1985-87	10.00	7.50
1983-84	7.50	6.00
before 1983	6.50	5.00

Price includes book rate postage within the U.S. For foreign orders, please add $1.00 per book. Fast United Parcel Service available within the U.S. at $2.50 for each order under $50.00, and calculated at 5% of invoice total for orders $50.00 or above.

All orders under $45.00 must be prepaid. Make check payable to ASHE-ERIC. For Visa or MasterCard, include card number, expiration date and signature. A bulk discount of 10% is available on orders of 15 or more books (not applicable on subscriptions).

Address order to
  ASHE-ERIC Higher Education Reports
  The George Washington University
  1 Dupont Circle, Suite 630
  Washington, DC 20036
Or phone (202) 296-2597
  Write for a complete catalog of ASHE-ERIC Higher Education Reports.

1990 ASHE-ERIC Higher Education Reports

1. The Campus Green: Fund Raising in Higher Education
   Barbara E. Brittingham and Thomas R. Pezzullo

2. The Emeritus Professor: Old Rank - New Meaning
   James E. Mauch, Jack W. Birch, and Jack Matthews

1989 ASHE-ERIC Higher Education Reports

1. Making Sense of Administrative Leadership: The 'L' Word in Higher Education
   Estela M. Bensimon, Anna Neumann, and Robert Birnbaum

2. Affirmative Rhetoric, Negative Action: African-American and Hispanic Faculty at Predominantly White Universities
   Valora Washington and William Harvey

3. Postsecondary Developmental Programs: A Traditional Agenda with New Imperatives
   Louise M. Tomlinson

4. The Old College Try: Balancing Athletics and Academics in Higher Education
   John R. Thelin and Lawrence L. Wiseman

5. The Challenge of Diversity: Involvement or Alienation in the Academy?
   Daryl G. Smith

6. Student Goals for College and Courses: A Missing Link in Assessing and Improving Academic Achievement
   Joan S. Stark, Kathleen M. Shaw, and Malcolm A. Lowther

7. The Student as Commuter: Developing a Comprehensive Institutional Response
   Barbara Jacoby

8. Renewing Civic Capacity: Preparing College Students for Service and Citizenship
   Suzanne W. Morse

1988 ASHE-ERIC Higher Education Reports

1. The Invisible Tapestry: Culture in American Colleges and Universities
   George D. Kuh and Elizabeth J. Whitt

2. Critical Thinking: Theory, Research, Practice, and Possibilities
   Joanne Gainen Kurfiss

3. Developing Academic Programs: The Climate for Innovation
   Daniel T. Seymour

4. Peer Teaching: To Teach is To Learn Twice
   Neal A. Whitman

5. Higher Education and State Governments: Renewed Partnership, Cooperation, or Competition?
   Edward R. Hines

6. Entrepreneurship and Higher Education: Lessons for Colleges, Universities, and Industry
   James S. Fairweather

7. Planning for Microcomputers in Higher Education: Strategies for the Next Generation
   Reynolds Ferrante, John Hayman, Mary Susan Carlson, and Harry Phillips

8. The Challenge for Research in Higher Education: Harmonizing Excellence and Utility
   Alan W. Lindsay and Ruth T. Neumann

1987 ASHE-ERIC Higher Education Reports

1. Incentive Early Retirement Programs for Faculty: Innovative Responses to a Changing Environment
   Jay L. Chronister and Thomas R. Kepple, Jr.

2. Working Effectively with Trustees: Building Cooperative Campus Leadership
   Barbara E. Taylor

3. Formal Recognition of Employer-Sponsored Instruction: Conflict and Collegiality in Postsecondary Education
   Nancy S. Nash and Elizabeth M. Hawthorne

4. Learning Styles: Implications for Improving Educational Practices
   Charles S. Claxton and Patricia H. Murrell

5. Higher Education Leadership: Enhancing Skills through Professional Development Programs
   Sharon A. McDade

6. Higher Education and the Public Trust: Improving Stature in Colleges and Universities
   Richard L. Alfred and Julie Weissman

7. College Student Outcomes Assessment: A Talent Development Perspective
   Maryann Jacobi, Alexander Astin, and Frank Ayala, Jr.

8. Opportunity from Strength: Strategic Planning Clarified with Case Examples
   Robert G. Cope

1986 ASHE-ERIC Higher Education Reports

1. Post-tenure Faculty Evaluation: Threat or Opportunity?
   Christine M. Licata

2. Blue Ribbon Commissions and Higher Education: Changing Academe from the Outside
   Janet R. Johnson and Laurence R. Marcus

3. Responsive Professional Education: Balancing Outcomes and Opportunities
   Joan S. Stark, Malcolm A. Lowther, and Bonnie M.K. Hagerty

4. Increasing Students' Learning: A Faculty Guide to Reducing Stress among Students
   Neal A. Whitman, David C. Spendlove, and Claire H. Clark

5. Student Financial Aid and Women: Equity Dilemma?
   Mary Moran

6. The Master's Degree: Tradition, Diversity, Innovation
   Judith S. Glazer

7. The College, the Constitution, and the Consumer Student: Implications for Policy and Practice
   Robert M. Hendrickson and Annette Gibbs

8. Selecting College and University Personnel: The Quest and the Question
   Richard A. Kaplowitz

1985 ASHE-ERIC Higher Education Reports

1. Flexibility in Academic Staffing: Effective Policies and Practices
   Kenneth P. Mortimer, Marque Bagshaw, and Andrew T. Masland

2. Associations in Action: The Washington, D.C. Higher Education Community
   Harland G. Bloland

3. And on the Seventh Day: Faculty Consulting and Supplemental Income
   Carol M. Boyer and Darrell R. Lewis

4. Faculty Research Performance: Lessons from the Sciences and Social Sciences
   John W. Creswell

5. Academic Program Review: Institutional Approaches, Expectations, and Controversies
   Clifton F. Conrad and Richard F. Wilson

6. Students in Urban Settings: Achieving the Baccalaureate Degree
   Richard C. Richardson, Jr. and Louis W. Bender

7. Serving More Than Students: A Critical Need for College Student Personnel Services
   Peter H. Garland

8. Faculty Participation in Decision Making: Necessity or Luxury?
   Carol E. Floyd

1984 ASHE-ERIC Higher Education Reports

1. Adult Learning: State Policies and Institutional Practices
   K. Patricia Cross and Anne-Marie McCartan

2. Student Stress: Effects and Solutions
   Neal A. Whitman, David C. Spendlove, and Claire H. Clark

3. Part-time Faulty: Higher Education at a Crossroads
   Judith M. Gappa

4. Sex Discrimination Law in Higher Education: The Lessons of
   the Past Decade. ED 252 169.*
   *J. Ralph Lindgren, Patti T. Ota, Perry A. Zirkel, and Nan Van
   Gieson*

5. Faculty Freedoms and Institutional Accountability: Interactions
   and Conflicts
   Steven G. Olswang and Barbara A. Lee

6. The High Technology Connection: Academic/Industrial Cooperation for Economic Growth
   Lynn G. Johnson

7. Employee Educational Programs: Implications for Industry and
   Higher Education. ED 258 501.*
   Suzanne W. Morse

8. Academic Libraries: The Changing Knowledge Centers of Colleges and Universities
   Barbara B. Moran

9. Futures Research and the Strategic Planning Process: Implications for Higher Education
   James L. Morrison, William L. Renfro, and Wayne I. Boucher

10. Faculty Workload: Research, Theory, and Interpretation
    Harold E. Yuker

1983 ASHE-ERIC Higher Education Reports

1. The Path to Excellence: Quality Assurance in Higher Education
   Laurence R. Marcus, Anita O. Leone, and Edward D. Goldberg

2. Faculty Recruitment, Retention, and Fair Employment: Ob-
   ligations and Opportunities
   John S. Waggaman

3. Meeting the Challenges: Developing Faculty Careers. ED 232
   516.*
   Michael C.T. Brooks and Katherine L. German

4. Raising Academic Standards: A Guide to Learning Improvement
   Ruth Talbott Keimig

5. Serving Learners at a Distance: A Guide to Program Practices
   Charles E. Feasley

*Out-of-print. Available through EDRS. Call 1-800-227-ERIC.

ALVERNO COLLEGE
INSTRUCTIONAL SERVICES CENTER

Quantity   **Amount**

_____ Please send a complete set of the 1989 *ASHE-ERIC Higher Education Reports* at $80.00, 33% off the cover price.   _____

_____ Please begin my subscription to the 1990 *ASHE-ERIC Higher Education Reports* at $80.00, 41% off the cover price, starting with Report 1, 1990   _____

_____ Outside the U.S., add $10 per series for postage   _____

Individual reports are avilable at the following prices:

1990 and forward, $17.00	1983 and 1984, $7.50
1988 and 1989, $15.00	1982 and back, $6.50
1985 to 1987, $10.00	

Book rate postage within the U.S. is included. Outside U.S., please add $1 per book for postage. Fast U.P.S. shipping is available within the U.S. at $2.50 for each order under $50.00, and calculated at 5% of invoice total for orders $50.00 or above. All orders under $45 must be prepaid.

PLEASE SEND ME THE FOLLOWING REPORTS:

Quantity	Report No.	Year	Title	Amount

Subtotal:

Foreign or UPS:

Total Due:

Please check one of the following:
- ☐ Check enclosed, payable to GWU-ERIC.
- ☐ Purchase order attached ($45.00 minimum).
- ☐ Charge my credit card indicated below:
  - ☐ Visa   ☐ MasterCard

Expiration Date _____

Name _____

Title _____

Institution _____

Address _____

City _____ State _____ Zip _____

Phone _____

Signature _____ Date _____

SEND ALL ORDERS TO:
ASHE-ERIC Higher Education Reports
The George Washington University
One Dupont Circle, Suite 630
Washington, DC 20036-1183
Phone: (202) 296-2597